ROME BEYOND
THE IMPERIAL FRONTIERS

Bronze statuette of Harpocrates from Taxila, Punjab. ¼ (*See p.* 158)

ROME
BEYOND THE
IMPERIAL FRONTIERS

BY

SIR MORTIMER WHEELER

Professor of the Archaeology of the Roman Provinces
in the University of London

GREENWOOD PRESS, PUBLISHERS
WESTPORT, CONNECTICUT

Originally published in 1954
by G. Bell and Sons, Ltd., London

Reprinted with the permission
of The Philosophical Library, Inc., New York

First Greenwood Reprinting 1971

Library of Congress Catalogue Card Number 70-139155

ISBN 0-8371-5771-4

Printed in the United States of America

PREFACE

THIS little book first took shape on a hot May morning in 1945, when an Indian student of mine emerged excitedly from a deep trench beside the Bay of Bengal waving a large slice of a red dish in his hand. Removal of the slimy sea-mud revealed the dish as a signed work of a potter whose kilns flourished nearly 2,000 years ago and 5,000 miles away, on the outskirts of Arezzo in Tuscany. Were drama admissible to the archaeological scene, I should have been tempted to describe the moment as dramatic. In that moment the pages of the historians and the geographers leapt to life; the long, acquisitive arm of imperial Rome became an actuality.

Elsewhere in the East, the discovery of Roman things, or their more local simulacra, has outpaced adequate record in recent years. The reason lies partly in the accident that few orientalists have been trained in the classical school, and that the significant Western material therefore, when found, is not always recognized. The present book does not profess to fulfil this need in any comprehensive sense. It is not an archaeological gazetteer, such as is now badly wanted; but it may at least serve summarily to indicate the scope of the problem and to invite further attention to those matters.

For the West, the field has been admirably surveyed, for some time to come, by Dr. H. J. Eggers in his monumental work on Roman imports into Free Germany, published while this book was in preparation. With Dr. Eggers's generous permission, I have drawn freely upon his material, particularly for my maps. To many others I am likewise greatly indebted for illustrations: especially to Dr. H. C. Broholm of Copenhagen, to Dr. G. Caputo, lately head of the Archaeological service in Libya, to Monsieur M. Reygasse of the Bardo, Algiers, to Mrs. Olwen Brogan and the Society for the Promotion of Roman Studies, to the Archaeological Department of the Government of India, to the late Director of the Baroda Museum and Picture Gallery, and to the German Archaeological Institute.

R. E. M. WHEELER

Institute of Archaeology,
    University of London, 1953

CONTENTS

PART III · ASIA

ILLUSTRATIONS

FIGURES IN THE TEXT

PLATES

I · INTRODUCTION

THIS book is concerned with Roman adventuring beyond the outermost boundaries of the Roman Empire. The subject is not new; its literature indeed, both ancient and modern, is immense; but there are new examples of it, and old material has recently been reviewed. In this adventuring Greek and Arab enterprise are wedded to the Roman faculty for exploitation. The boundaries of the Empire, particularly in the East, were sufficiently fluid to ensure a constant awareness of more distant horizons, of greater riches, more marvels, fresh menaces. A century and a quarter before Trajan's thrust to the further bank of the Tigris, Maecenas at Rome, as Horace tells us, was 'fearing what the Seres [Chinese or Central Asians] may be plotting, and Bactra once ruled by Cyrus, and the discordant tribes on the banks of Tanais [Jaxartes]'. Nor was this a merely academic fear. 'The credit of the Roman money-market', said Cicero, 'is intimately bound up with the prosperity of Asia. A disaster cannot occur there without shaking our credit to its foundations.' The term 'Asia' had to Cicero a limited implication, but the dictum was broadly true. On the European frontiers the commercial element was, from the Roman standpoint, less insistent; nevertheless, un-conquered Germany remained a recurrent source of anxiety or, at its mildest, a stimulus to Roman interest and curiosity.

At the outset the word 'Roman' requires definition. It is not indeed closely definable, particularly when applied to trade. The Italian was no great sailor, just as he was no great horseman, and not a little of the trafficking beyond the frontiers involved the use of ships. Therein both fo'c'sle and quarterdeck must, more often than not, have been manned by Frisians, Greeks, Levantines, Arabs and others who, like Kipling's Parnesius, had 'never seen Rome except in a picture'. For the present purpose all these folk will pass muster as 'Romans', so be it that they were directly in the service of Imperial commerce. There shall be no great pedantry here in the matter of race or colour or even citizenship.

And as to geography, the widest Imperial limits of the 2nd century A.D. are assumed as our base-line (*end map*). Else, for example, we had need to remind the reader of the Roman traders who in the 1st centuries B.C. and A.D. preceded the flag in Gallia Comata or Belgic Britain, with tiresome argument as to Cunobelin's foreign moneyers and the extent of his own part in the cross-Channel trade that littered his squalid huts at Colchester with fine Arretine dishes or brought silver goblets to pre-Claudian Welwyn.

Nor are we concerned here with the sporadic pervasion of goods from Roman Britain into the outlands of Scotland or Ireland. Scraps of pottery and occasionally more spectacular wares reached the native homesteads of Scotland,[1] and are there useful mainly for dating undemonstrative local cultures. A more restricted scatter in Ireland occasionally has a similar use; as at Tara, where Professor Seán Ó Ríordáin has dug up sherds of 3rd-century Roman vessels, brought by traders or (more likely) raiders to this famous seat of kings.[2]

The bulk of our matter falls into two zones, the European and the Asiatic. A third is beginning to emerge in the deserts of North Africa, where there is accumulating evidence that the traders who brought ivory northwards across the Sahara to the coastal cities of Libya carried back Roman goods far into the interior; and though this fact may not be one of far-reaching historical significance, the importations have at least a value archaeologically as a potential means of dating associated African cultures. The East African coast,

---

[1] For an account of these strays, as known in 1932, see J. Curle, 'An Inventory of Objects of Roman and Provincial Roman Origin found on Sites in Scotland not definitely associated with Roman Constructions', *Proceedings of the Society of Antiquaries of Scotland*, LXVI (1932), 277-397.

[2] For Roman goods found in Ireland prior to 1948, see S. P. Ó Ríordáin in *Proceedings of the Royal Irish Academy* (Section C), LI (1948), 35-82. The sherds from Tara were found in 1952-3.

another likely region for Roman contacts, is at present virtually unexplored.

Our evidence in the following pages will be of two main kinds. First there are extensive and largely familiar references to this trans-frontier venturing in the classical and Asian records. Secondly, there are numerous discoveries of Roman or Graeco-Roman commodities, or of native goods reflecting classical influences, in lands without the Empire. Most, though not all, of the literary references have a commercial context. The material 'finds', whether in Free Germany or in further Asia, are often more difficult to interpret. A majority of them, especially in India or Indo-China, are manifestly the products of trade or at least of commercial drift. A minority may be explained as the fruits of war; as when the three legions under Varus were overwhelmed by the German tribesmen in A.D. 9 and lost their whole vast equipment to the victors. Other objects of value found their way across the borders as propitiatory gifts to native princes; as in our own time golden sovereigns, for example, have flowed diplomatically into Arabia. Again, tribal movement across or along the frontiers of Central Europe must have involved a displacement of Roman things on a fairly considerable scale. By and large, the problem of interpretation is not a simple one. It must be discussed at later stages in the light of individual circumstance.

But, when all is said, trade will be discovered as the dominant factor in these remote contacts. The Roman traders and their agents were venturesome folk, whether we regard the enterprising knight who in the time of Nero made his way to the Baltic and brought back a great load of amber, or the pioneers who in the 2nd century reopened the trans-Asian 'Silk Route' beyond Tashkurgan, or again those others who in A.D. 166 carried gifts to the emperor of China and so opened or reopened a sea-way to the Far East. Amber, pearls, pepper, silk, such were the goals of all this trafficking, and most of it is of interest to us to-day in the

sense that perilous voyaging and travellers' tales are of
perennial interest to those who care for human enterprise.
But once at least this trafficking did something more than
merely scatter Roman bric-à-brac across the world. In
Afghanistan and what is now West Pakistan it was the
instrument of a cultural contact which had a far-reaching
effect upon the history of art.

It stands to reason that the surviving vestiges of this
interchange are in kind but a fraction of the whole, and
that their survival is fraught with all manner of accident.
The slaves and hunting-dogs and corn imported into the
Roman world from Britain; the cotton cloth from India;
the wine that flowed into Free Germany or was borne by the
monsoon to the tables of Indian princes; the 'Seric' skins from
High Asia, the silk from China; the spice that filled the
Pepper Barns of Rome; for these and much else we have
to rely almost entirely upon chance scraps of history. In
the circumstances, the surprising thing is not how little but
how much has survived in the form of material evidence.
Roman coinage reached India in quantity and even penetrated to Indo-China. Roman glass has been recorded
from the Trondheim fiord on the one hand and (admittedly
with less certainty) from Honan and Korea on the other.
Silver cups from Italy and the provinces equipped the graves
of the native nobility in Germany, Czechoslovakia, Poland
and Denmark. Bronze vessels reached Norway and western
India. To western India again, and to Afghanistan, came
Roman bronze figurines, and others have been recovered
from the native homestead-mounds of the Low Countries.
Red-glazed pottery from Italy or the western provinces is
found alike in Poland and on the Coromandel Coast.
Roman arms and armour were dedicated in the meres of
Jutland. The list might be extended, and will in due course
be dealt with categorically. Meanwhile, enough has been
said to indicate its range.

From this point, the book will be divided into three parts,
dealing respectively with Europe, Africa, and Asia. Europe will

for our purpose comprise Free Germany (including Scandinavia) ; Africa will be subdivided into the Sahara and the East Coast; Asia will include the Indo-Pakistan sub-continent and Afghanistan on the one hand, and the Far East on the other. Two important regions are omitted: Russia, and the variable eastern frontier with Persia. For both, much further ground-work is needed. The latter in particular, with its rich historical background and the incessant military, political, and cultural interaction which, for example, brought Mithraism and Manichaeism to Europe and immortalized the ignominy of three Roman emperors on the crags of Bishapur and Naqsh-i-Rustam[1] now demands a particular and extensive study beyond the scope of the present book. Such study, when undertaken, will produce a strange *mélange* of thought and form, including incidentally a surprising manifestation of Celtic art from the Rhineland in 3rd-century Dura beside the Euphrates. But whether the long-range traffic which contributed to the prosperity of Palmyra and her satellite ports on the Persian Gulf ever approached in significance that of Alexandria, of which something will be said in a later chapter, seems increasingly doubtful. Judgement must remain open pending the fuller evaluation of work such as that now in progress at Hatra and, above all, a comprehensive publication of the material from Palmyra itself.

1. B. C. MacDermot, 'Roman emperors in the Sassanian reliefs', *Journ. of Roman Studies*, XLIV (1954), 76.

* * *

II · FREE GERMANY
THE LITERARY EVIDENCE

BEFORE the middle of the 1st century B.C. hardy Roman business-men were already operating amidst the German tribes across the Rhine. 'The Suebi', Caesar tells us (*De Bello Gallico*, IV, 1-3), 'by far the largest and most warlike nation amongst the Germans, give access to traders, rather to secure buyers for what they have captured in war than to satisfy any craving for imports.' The Suebi were an amalgam of German tribes who, in the time of Strabo (late 1st century B.C.) were living between the Rhine and the Elbe, and in that of Tacitus, about A.D. 98, were occupying 'more than half Germany'; more precisely, north-western Germany and the middle and lower Rhine as far as the sea. Caesar adds that 'they suffer no importation of wine whatsoever, believing that men are thereby rendered too soft and womanish for the endurance of hardship'. This remark implies that elsewhere wine was an acceptable import; Tacitus (*Germania*, 23) states that 'the Germans who live nearest the Rhine can actually get wine in the market', whilst those in the interior 'extract a juice from barley or grain, which is fermented to make something not unlike wine'. Roman wine-vessels from the Jutland Peninsula are found to have contained a fermented drink made from malt and berry-juice, recalling the cranberry wine, mixed with myrtle and honey, of which desiccated remains are found already in Danish burials of the Bronze Age, over 1,000 years earlier. Caesar does not tell us what the Roman traders gave in exchange for surplus Suebian loot, but it may be supposed that silver money and Roman metalwork formed, now as later, a part of the apparatus.

Certainly by the 1st century A.D. Roman silver coinage was an established factor in the German trade. Again Tacitus is our historian (*Germ.* 5): 'The Germans nearest us value gold and silver for their use in trade, and recognize and prefer certain types of Roman money. (The peoples of the interior, truer to the plain old ways, employ barter.) They like money that is old and familiar, *denarii* with the notched edge and the type of two-horse chariot. Another point is that they try to get silver in preference to gold. They have no predilection for the metal, but find plenty of silver change more serviceable in buying cheap and common goods.' The distribution-map (fig. 6) shows that by the 3rd century Roman coinage had spread into Germany far beyond the vicinity of the *limes*. The preference for the older types of silver obviously derives from the dilution of the *denarius* by Nero, and reflects the native use of the money, not as a token currency backed by a state guarantee (for there could be none such beyond the frontier), but as so much bullion of honest intrinsic worth. That intrinsic worth was permanently impaired by the monetary 'reform' of A.D. 63. More will be said of this matter in a later chapter (p. 63).

The early trade across the frontiers was not without its dangers to the adventurers who undertook it. Some thirty years after Caesar's casual reference to Roman traders amongst the Suebi, the legate of Augustus 'took vengeance on certain Celts [i.e. Germans] because they had arrested and slain Romans who entered their country to trade with them' (Dio, LIII, 26). Such vicissitudes were doubtless a part of the day's work. On the whole, however, it is to be assumed that this trafficking was welcome enough on both sides. Thus in A.D. 18, as Tacitus tells us (*Annals*, II, 62), there were domiciled at the capital of the king of the Marcomanni, i.e. in Bohemia, a number of sutlers and traders 'implanted first on foreign soil by commercial privileges, then by the lure of increased profits, and finally by oblivion of their country'. The king, Maroboduus, had himself been to Italy in his earlier days and doubtless encouraged this trade as a matter of policy and as a demonstration of enlightenment. Tacitus is reinforced by the distribution-maps (e.g. fig. 7), which show in the earlier part of the 1st century, but rarely afterwards, a concentration of Roman relics in the Marcomannian area. This area was approached most readily from the neighbouring 'amber route', which left the Danube at Carnuntum and penetrated up the tributary valley of the March towards the German plain and the Baltic.

The route to the Baltic is itself the subject of a well-known episode recounted by Pliny (*Natural History*, XXXVII, 45). In the time of Nero a Roman knight, agent of a certain Julianus, made the arduous journey to the Baltic coast, where he visited *commercia* or agencies, and eventually returned, presumably by way of East Prussia and Poland, with a great quantity of amber. The pioneering character of this journey implies that previously the northern sectors of the amber traffic had been in unrestricted native hands, and the knight, though primarily concerned, it seems, with the equipment of gladiatorial shows for Nero, may well have been prospecting incidentally with a view to simplifying the trade and reducing its costs. We would give much for a sight of his report.

Commercial enterprise was not all one way. Tacitus (*Germ.* 41) states that the tribe of the Hermunduri, who lay to the north of the upper Danube as far as Thuringia, 'are the only Germans who trade with us, not only on the river-bank, but deep inside our lines, in the brilliant colony that is the capital of Raetia. They come over where they will, and without a guard. To other nations we only show off our arms and our camps; to them we expose our palaces and our country-mansions—and they do not covet them.' Free trade of this kind may not in fact have been quite as rare as Tacitus affirms. Much later, after the defeat of the insurgent Marcomanni in A.D. 173, Marcus Aurelius 'established the places and the days for their trading, for these had not been previously fixed' (Dio, LXXII, 15). Whatever the custom on the Rhine, traffic across the Danube frontier would appear to have been substantially unregulated until the disturbances of the latter half of the 2nd century.

Trade apart, Roman things reached Germany through war and through diplomacy. For the latter two references from the *Germania* (5 and 42) are in point: 'One may see among them [the Germans] silver vessels which have been given as presents to their envoys and chiefs'; and again, 'the might and power of the kings [of the Marcomanni and the Quadi] depend upon the authority of Rome. These kings occasionally receive our armed assistance, more often our financial, and it is equally effective'. It may be assumed indeed that diplomatic bribery was a normal feature of the relationships between Rome and Free Germany, and helped very materially in the scattering of coinage and other valuables. Thus when, about A.D. 90, Chariomerus, pro-Roman king of the Cherusci, was driven from his kingdom by the Chatti, he appealed to Domitian and 'did not secure any military aid but received money' (Dio, LXVII, 5). And Decebalus, king of the Dacians, was bought off both by lavish payments and also by the receipt of technical aid. About A.D. 89 Domitian sought to keep him quiet by sending 'large sums of money and artisans of every trade, both peaceful and warlike, and promised to keep on giving large sums in future' (Dio, LXVII, 7). This subvention was continued for 10 years or more, and one of the reasons for Trajan's campaign against the Dacians was his anxiety 'at the amount of money they were receiving annually' (Dio, LXVIII, 15). The submission of the Dacian king in A.D. 102 included the surrender of his 'arms, engines and engine-makers' (Dio, LXVIII, 9), presumably the Roman technicians seconded to him by Domitian. But the flow of coinage across the frontier increased rather than diminished as time went on. The Roman gold which was freely distributed in barbarian Europe in the time of the Goths and, above all, the Huns reflects in part the continuance of this policy on an exaggerated scale at the lower limit of our period.

III · FREE GERMANY
ROUTES AND MARKETS

BEFORE we pass from the historical to the material evidence for this interchange, something may be said of the principal areas and routes with which our study is concerned. To do this at so early a stage is of course to reverse the logical sequence, and to anticipate the map-patterns which are found to emerge from the inquiry. But the active work of Scandinavian and German scholars during the past few decades has rendered this inverted procedure possible, and it is justifiable on the ground that a summary survey such as the present is more readily intelligible if the geographical aspects are sketched in at the outset.

First let it be said that no special attention is given here to the occurrence of Roman things within a belt fifty miles wide outside the formal frontier or *limes*. A marginal spread of this kind speaks for itself and can here be simultaneously defined and dismissed. In the time of Hadrian, the frontier on which it was based extended up the Rhine nearly to Coblenz, then bore eastwards in a great salient round the Taunus, southwards into Württemberg, and eastwards again to the Danube above Regensburg. Thence it followed the Danube to the Black Sea, save where it bent northwards to the Carpathians to enclose the province of Dacia. This broad frontier-zone across Europe frames on the south and west the Free Germany with which the present chapter deals. In the north and east, that Germany is regarded as extending to Norway, Sweden, Latvia, Poland and South Russia, without any attempted discrimination of racial and linguistic boundaries, which must indeed have been numerous and sometimes formidable. The whole vast region was an *officina gentium*, a welter of nations increasingly mobile as

the Imperial era wore on, already sufficiently kaleidoscopic
before the mongoloid Huns brought final chaos into it at the
end of the 4th century.   In the circumstances it need scarcely
be emphasized that the term 'free' is here merely a euphem-
ism for 'outside the formal boundaries of the Roman Empire
in the 2nd century A.D.', i.e. the boundaries defined above,
always with the reservation that those boundaries were
extensively withdrawn by the rupture of the Rhine-Danube
limes in A.D. 258-260 and the surrender of Dacia beyond the
Danube a dozen years later.

ROUTES

Far beyond the range of mere frontier-diffusion a number
of main routes carried goods to and from the depths of this
Free Germany (fig. 1), and the arterial traffic was supplemented
by lateral pervasions which tend to blur the map-pattern and
complicate its interpretation.   Within the Empire the traffic
was focused on three great regions: Italy, Gaul with the
German provinces, and the periphery of the Black Sea.   Of
these, the first to dominate the scene was naturally Italy;
but in the 2nd century A.D. the developing industries of Gaul
and the Rhineland were of increasing importance, and in the
3rd century probably outstripped Italy in their trans-frontier
influence.   Shortly after the middle of that century, the
tribal confederacy known as the Goths, who had long been
moving southwards from their Baltic homeland, encom-
passed the northern and western shores of the Black Sea and
now became an instrument in the diffusion of the rich
craftsmanship of Byzantium, South Russia and the Near
East towards barbarian Europe.   Trade, conquest, subvention, drift, all contributed to the complex process of
dispersal and are usually hard to discriminate.   But in one
way and another, by the 3rd and 4th centuries Gaul and the
lands of the Black Sea had between them largely replaced
Italy as the sources of classical craftsmanship in Free Germany,
whilst subsequently the Eastern Empire of Byzantium

became the major factor.   Of all this complex trade and movement through four centuries, the principal lines of intercourse

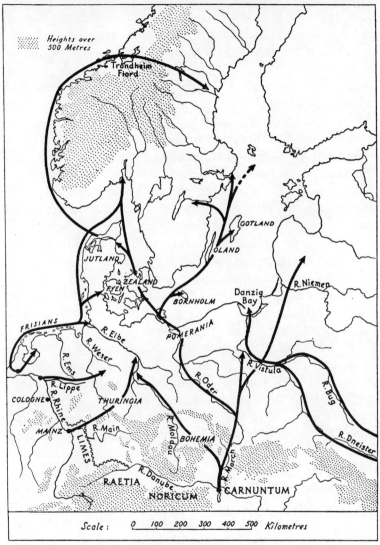

Fig. 1   Principal European trade-routes

and the principal termini are tolerably clear; only the
motives and occasions are, more often than not, held from us.

From Italy in the first two centuries A.D. came, above all, bronze wares and glass. Of both, Campania was probably the foremost producer, although the accidental preponderance of material from the Campanian cities of Herculaneum and Pompeii tends to distort our perspective. At any rate, Aquileia at the head of the Adriatic was the chief point of assembly; it was inevitably Aquileia, for instance, that became the goal of the insurgent Marcomanni and their allies when they burst through the Julian Alps in A.D. 167. No doubt the tribesmen followed well-trodden trade-routes between the Danube and Aquileia, in particular the high-road built by Augustus through the province of Noricum (Austria) and Upper Pannonia to the Danubian fortress of Carnuntum, placed strategically at the junction with the March below Vienna. Noricum itself developed metal industries with local characters which can be recognized in graves far away in Jutland, and was clearly not blind to the strategic possibilities of its position.

From Carnuntum an early route led northwards up the valley of the March, forking westwards into Bohemia or continuing northwards through the Moravian Gates into the German plain. There it struck the upper reaches of the Oder, but soon branched northwards again towards Kalisz in western Poland and so reached the lower Vistula and the Amber Coast of the Baltic, which was its main objective. Traffic along this ancient route—indeed, long-distance traffic of the kind in any part of Free Germany—must have been a matter of constant relay with accumulating dues, and it has been suggested above that the exploratory journey of the knight of Julianus in Nero's reign was in part an attempt to simplify and cheapen the process. By whatever means, throughout the period with which we are dealing Roman things circulated fairly constantly through this natural artery from the lands tapped by the Danube if not always from Italy itself. Roman coins of the 2nd century reached the lips of the dead in the neighbourhood of Königsberg, bronze vessels of the 2nd and 3rd centuries were entombed in the lands south and west of Danzig Bay, and in the 4th and 5th centuries Roman gold bestrewed the Amber Coast and the Swedish islands as token of the new, uneasy partnership of barbarism with the civilized world.

The western branch-route from the March into Bohemia had only an intermittent importance, but was more instrumental than any other known route in opening up central Europe to Roman trade in the early days of the Empire. The historical position of Bohemia, home of the powerful Marcomanni and their neighbours the Quadi, is sufficiently outstanding to demand a short historical excursus at a later stage. Meanwhile, it will suffice to observe that in the early decades of the 1st century A.D. Bohemia was a leading entrepôt of Roman trade in Free Germany and must have been instrumental in the diffusion of Roman goods northwards into Prussia and beyond; that by the middle of the century this trade had diminished to vanishing point; but that some sort of revival took place under the later Empire, when coinage and bronze-wares again reached the region in modest quantities. Bohemia and Silesia contain natural resources, notably tin, of value to the classical world, but the independent spirit of the local tribesmen in their secluded and forested highland homes was an obstruction to regular interchange.

Another approach into and through Bohemia from the Danube valley lay from the vicinity of Linz across to the Moldau and via Prague, Dresden, Meissen, Leipzig and Halle to the Elbe, the German Plain, the Jutland peninsula and Scandinavia. The route was, in part at any rate, an old one, but as a whole its importance in the Roman period appears to represent a secondary development and never to have rivalled that of more easterly and more westerly alternatives.

In the west, sea-routes and land-routes combined to supply western Germany and the Baltic lands. The sea-routes are necessarily less sensitive to archaeological recognition but must not on that account be underrated. In the proud record of Augustus at Ankara it is proclaimed that

'My fleet made an ocean voyage from the mouth of the Rhine to the eastward as far as the boundaries of the Cimbri whither before that time no Roman had penetrated either by land or by sea; and the Cimbri, the Charydes, the Semnones and other German peoples of that same region sent emissaries to seek my friendship and that of the Roman People'. These were tribes of the Elbe valley and the Jutland peninsula, though whether the fleet circumnavigated the peninsula on this occasion may be doubted. The Romans were timid sailors, and it may be supposed that the longshore tribes, above all the Frisians of the Dutch coast, became the principal carriers of the subsequent sea-borne trade hereabouts. Their main markets towards the north-east lay in Jutland, where amber was procurable, and in the populous Danish islands; and a short land-route across the base of the peninsula between the North Sea and the western Baltic may be presumed. Trans-peninsular routes were a normal substitute for circumnavigation in ancient times, and a more ambitious example within the 1st century A.D. will emerge when we review the evidence from South India (p. 144).

By land, the eastern tributaries of the Rhine offered access from the Roman frontier to Westphalia and Thuringia. The Lippe, with the fortress of Vetera (Xanten) at its base, the Ruhr from Asciburgium, less certainly the Sieg from Bonn, all played some part in this traffic; above all, perhaps the Lahn and the Main, the latter overlooked by the key-fortress at Mainz. These valley-routes tended to converge upon Paderborn in eastern Westphalia and the Weser-crossings at Minden, Hameln and Höxter, whence dispersal into the broad lowlands towards the Elbe and even to the Baltic was not difficult.

South of Mainz the country east of the frontier becomes more broken and rugged, and clear traces of arterial traffic cease. Nevertheless, the province of Raetia, overlapping the upper waters of the Danube, must have acted in some measure as a link between Upper Germany and Gaul on the one hand and the Danubian axis on the other, and there are hints that pottery (*terra sigillata* and 'Rhenish' ware) and other objects from western factories occasionally passed this way. But the main commercial activity of Raetia was directed historically towards the north. There in the 1st century A.D. lay the considerable nation of the Hermunduri, whose whereabouts at various periods has given rise to considerable argument[1] and doubtless, indeed, fluctuated with the characteristic mobility of the German tribesmen. They are strangely ignored by the geographer Ptolemy about A.D. 150, but were placed by Strabo (end of the 1st century B.C.) east of the Elbe. On the other hand, between 7 and 3 B.C. Ahenobarbus, commander on the upper Danube, had penetrated as far as the Elbe or the Saale and, in doing so, had (according to Dio, LV, 10*a*) 'intercepted the Hermunduri, a tribe which for some reason or other had left their own land and were wandering about in search of another'. He settled them on territory vacated by the Marcomanni when they moved from the neighbourhood of the Main and the Neckar to Bohemia (see below, p. 19). The name of the Hermunduri has been connected philologically with Thuringia, but, though they appear to have occupied that region during some part of their history, the identification cannot be sustained. Tacitus, as we have seen, places them nearly 100 miles further south, describing them as 'the only Germans who trade with us . . . deep inside our lines, in the brilliant colony that is the capital of Raetia' (p. 9). We may perhaps recognize a northern and a southern branch of the tribe, one in Thuringia and the Saale-Elbe valley, the other, presumably coterminous, in Bavaria round about Nuremberg. Archaeology emphasizes the commercial importance of Thuringia, beside a traditional route between the Baltic and the west, but offers no clear illustration of the statement of Tacitus in regard to Raetia. Its reticence in this matter is a sufficient reminder of the incompleteness of our picture in times or regions where history fails us.

If we turn eastwards again, to modern Hungary or ancient

[1] Reviewed in *Germania*, XXIII (1939), 262ff.

Dacia and as far east as South Russia and the environs of the Black Sea, we find ourselves in lands which have been inadequately explored and are at the present time inaccessible. East of Budapest the valley of the Theiss marked a route northwards from the Danube to the Carpathian passes and so into Galicia and central Poland and on to the Baltic—a route which may be supposed to have shared in the amber trade but can scarcely have depended wholly upon it. Then, still further east, the rich environs of the Black Sea, important to us in the later 3rd and 4th centuries, were tapped by the valleys of the Dniester and the Dnieper, the former pointing to Galicia and the Vistula or the Oder, the latter to White Russia and the south-eastern Baltic. There can be little doubt that with ampler knowledge these eastern routes would be found to rival the better-known arteries of the west; the heavy distribution-pattern of 4th- and 5th-century finds, mostly from the Eastern Empire, on the Swedish islands and the East Prussian coast is sufficiently significant.

MARKETS

From routes we turn to the markets which they supplied, and in doing so encounter at once the initial handicap to which reference has been made above: the vicissitudes of survival. Nevertheless, it seems likely that the principal regions of concentration on our maps are reasonably representative, if by no means complete. Of the somewhat left-handed trade which, as Caesar tells us (p. 7), the Suebi of north-western Germany encouraged in the 1st century B.C., there is no recognizable vestige unless certain Italic or Italo-Gaulish bronze vessels of that general period found in cremation-burials of the Weser-Elbe zone (Eggers, map 3; see Bibliography, p. 182) are attributed to it. For a majority of these vessels, however, an approach from the south-east via the upper valley of the Oder is more likely. On the other hand, Bohemia, land of the Marcomanni and the Quadi, comes appropriately on to the map during the early decades of the 1st century A.D., in historical circumstances which may be recalled.

Bohemia. 'Next to the Hermunduri dwell the Naristi, followed by the Marcomanni and the Quadi. The Marcomanni are conspicuous in renown and power; they won the very land they now hold by their bravery, when they drove out the Boii. . . . The might and power of the kings depend upon the authority of Rome. These kings occasionally received our armed assistance, more often our financial, and it is equally effective.' So Tacitus (*Germ.* 42). It would appear that the Marcomanni were originally settled in the valleys of the Main and Neckar, whence in the time of Caesar they took arms with his opponent Ariovistus; but in 9 B.C. Drusus, a few weeks before his death, launched an attack upon them, with the important consequence that they migrated eastwards to the uplands of Bohemia. There, in country at the same time fertile and sufficiently difficult to discourage interference from the west or south, they occupied the old home of the Boii and quickly developed into a dominant native power.

Their leader in this phase of migration and aggrandisement was the celebrated king Maroboduus, who knew Rome and may actually have served with the Roman army. His knowledge enabled him both to deal with Roman diplomacy and to apply his Roman training to the organization and defence of his own large kingdom. His strength and ambition were not underrated by his opponents. A careful and skilful policy of encirclement culminated in A.D. 4 in a threefold thrust into his country—from Mainz, from Raetia and from Illyricum—and his last-moment escape was due only to a timely revolt in Illyricum behind the advance. The frustrate campaign ended in a treaty whereby Maroboduus was acclaimed a friend of the Roman people. But, where Rome had failed to tread, Maroboduus's fellow Germans stepped in and won the day. From the north, Bohemia is penetrated by the upper valley of the Elbe and its tributary the Moldau. Up these valleys in A.D. 18 streamed a host of rival tribes under the leadership of

Arminius who, since his grim victory over Varus in A.D. 9, had been the champion of German freedom. The threat was more than even the power and prestige of Maroboduus could withstand; and when Arminius received support from an exiled Marcomannian, a certain Catualda, bringing at least diplomatic encouragement from Rome, the king himself fled to his double-dealing Roman friends, to end his days, years later, in sanctuary at Ravenna.

Tacitus, it will be recalled (p. 8), tells us that, when Catualda entered the capital of the vanquished Maroboduus, he found a number of Roman traders in residence there, operating under commercial privileges which had presumably been included in the treaty of A.D. 4. That treaty may be supposed to have regularized an existing state of affairs rather than to have initiated a new one. Roman traders, like those of ascendant powers in later ages, were ever wont to precede the flag, and the Roman training of Maroboduus must have inclined him to encourage them, with or without a formal writ. Be that as it may, Italic bronze vessels of the first half of the 1st century A.D. are at home in Bohemia (fig. 7), together with a considerable coinage, mainly of silver, but including gold; and from Bohemia these imports spread northwards by the river valleys to the North Sea and the Baltic.

There is evidence that at this early period the Marcomanni played something of a creative role in the development of central European craftsmanship. Geographically and ethnically they were indeed in a favourable position to do so. Coming from the west, they were in contact with the Celtic world; they looked northwards to the German plain and Scandinavia; partially romanized Noricum (Austria) was at their doorstep; Roman agents were in their midst. They fell thus under a number of diverse stimuli and for a brief time formed a sort of cultural exchange and mart.[1] Thus

[1] See a discussion by O. Almgren, 'Zur Bedeutung des Markomannen-reiches in Böhmen für die Entwicklung der germanischen Industrie in das frühen Kaizerzeit', in *Mannus*, V (Würzburg, 1913), 255-78.

A. Silver cup from a 'chieftain's' grave at Hoby, Laaland. ½ (*See p.* 37)

B. Silver cup, partially gilt, from a 'chieftain's' grave at Dollerup, Denmark. ⅔ (*See p.* 40)

Bronze jug from a 'chieftain's' grave at Hoby, Laaland. ⅔
(*See p.* 37)

certain types of brooch and belt-fittings, particularly with stylized animal-heads, are common to Bohemia and Noricum. On the other hand, a well-known type of brooch with two piercings or circles ('eyes') on the head of the bow—a late La Tène type which in subsequent forms was to become characteristic of the Rhineland—came in from the opposite direction, from Brandenburg, Posen and Saxony, and was developed in Bohemia, whence it passed to the Rhine after the collapse of the Maroboduus régime. And it was seemingly in Bohemia that many of the earlier drinking-horns of this period were made, to judge from the fact that there, within a restricted territory, occur all the earliest known types of bronze fittings which are elsewhere scattered sporadically from the Rhine to Gotland. It was an established custom amongst the Germans to supply their drinking-horns with metal rims and terminals and to equip them with chains or straps for suspension; in the words of Caesar (*B.G.* VI, 28): 'They zealously collect the horns and encase the edges with silver, and then at their grandest banquets use them as drinking-cups.' Examples will be mentioned later (pp. 36, 39, 42).

After the exile of Maroboduus, Italo-Bohemian commerce rapidly deteriorated. The latest Roman gold coin from Bohemia during the 1st century is a solitary *aureus* of Titus (A.D. 79-81), and the general run of imports had ceased nearly half a century before that date. The consolidation of Roman authority in southern and western Europe had opened up alternative routes and markets, and the Bohemian tribes, increasingly isolated and (it may be) overcrowded, were becoming restive. An uneasy peace, interrupted momentarily at the time of Domitian's Dacian war by a firm Roman diplomacy, itself bordering upon war, ended in A.D. 167, when the Marcomannian king Ballomar led his tribesmen and allies across the Danube, defeated a Roman army, and besieged the pivotal market-town of Aquileia on the Adriatic. The Roman emperor reacted with determination; the invaders were beaten back, and in 172 Marcus

c

Aurelius led his forces to victory against the Quadi, on the eastern flank of the Marcomanni. In the following year came the turn of the Marcomanni themselves. Their territory was occupied and a part of the population was transported.[1] Thereafter they never again so nearly threatened the safety of Rome, but they did not cease to contribute to the recurrent restlessness of the Danube frontier, and such trade as lingered on was canalized and constrained by Roman treaty.[2] Only in the latter part of the 4th century did gold coinage and bronze vessels again find their way to Bohemia in appreciable quantity, at a time when eastern Europe was in the grip of the Huns.

Thuringia. Between the Thuringian Forest and the Elbe, in a rough triangle formed by Erfurt, Leipzig and Magdeburg and extending into the Forest, a concentration of coins, particularly of the Middle Empire, is less easy to explain. With them are vessels of bronze, pottery and glass, the two last certainly from the west. They presumably arrived in part by the river-routes from the Rhineland (p. 16), above all perhaps by an old way from Mainz over the Wetterau, continued in and beyond Thuringia by the valleys of the Saale and the Elbe. This was, incidentally, the line of a prehistoric amber-route from Jutland to the middle Rhine; a route which, until chaos supervened in the latter half of the 3rd century A.D., alternatively continued south-eastwards up the Elbe to Bohemia and the Danube, and so connected Thuringia with Noricum and the eastern traffic-system. Furthermore, if the Hermunduri extended to Thuringia, we have the clear witness of Tacitus (p. 9) for active intercourse more directly with the south, with the province of Raetia. Thuringia would thus appear to have occupied something of a nodal point in European trade. It is at least certain that, in a fertile region accessible though at the same

---

[1] Dio, LXXII, II, 4, refers to a revolt of Marcomanni settled at Ravenna, where, incidentally, Maroboduus had been given sanctuary over a century and a half previously (see above). After the revolt, Marcus evicted the settlers.

[2] Marcus 'established the places and the days for their trading (for these had not been previously fixed)'. Dio, LXXII, 15.

time screened by a succession of massifs and woods, the Thuringians or Hermunduri developed a liking for Roman things of which some account will be given in later sections.

The Baltic Coast and Eastern Europe. A thickening of Roman goods in the approaches to the gulf of Danzig (e.g. fig. 12) draws attention to the geographical importance of East Prussia and its environs in the commercial and political picture of the period. Historically our information is of the scantiest, although the wealth of the Pomeranian-East Prussian coast in amber, and the popularity of amber in the ancient world, are established facts. Pliny's reference, already cited (p. 9), to a Roman knight who, in the time of Nero, set out on an exploratory journey from Carnuntum to the Baltic coast and returned with a great quantity of amber merely underlines familiar knowledge.

But if history fails us, archaeology has produced some significant results. The coin-evidence is particularly striking. A majority of the individual Roman coins from East Prussia have been found in graves, which have produced upwards of 559 of them (Bolin; see p. 63, footnote 3), mostly *sesterces*. By far the greatest number of the coin-graves has been found north-east of the gulf of Danzig, in the coastland between the rivers Pregel and Niemen, but they extend southwards to the old border with Poland and Russia, where their apparent cessation may be due merely to lack of research. In some graves the coins were introduced as ornaments, but in others they had been placed between the lips of the dead, the Charon's fee of the classical world. Save in Samland where more than half of the coins are earlier than A.D. 138, a large majority of them date from A.D. 138 to 180 (the accession of the emperor Commodus), and in Samland itself of four hoards of *sesterces* three end with Commodus and the fourth with Septimius Severus. The second half of the 2nd century was evidently the optimum period.

Before conclusions are drawn from this concentration of coinage, one overriding factor must be considered: namely, the circumstances of the preservation of the coins. Be it repeated that most of them have been found in graves. The prerequisite condition is that the inhabitants of the region concerned were in the habit of including coins amongst their grave-goods. Similar coins may well have circulated just as freely amongst a neighbouring people whose funerary fashions were of a different sort. And that such was almost certainly the case has been demonstrated by Eggers with the aid of two maps of the Vistula-Baltic region (fig. 2). One map shows the coin-distribution just recounted; the other shows the distribution of Roman bronze vessels found in the graves of the same area. The one map is almost exactly the complement of the other; where the coin-burials end, the burials with bronze vessels begin. The inference is not in doubt. In fact we are confronted, not with the vagaries of Roman trade, but with those of native burial-custom. The lesson is one to bear in mind in instances where the materials for such demonstration may not be available.

To the further obvious question, What ancient frontier— cultural or political—does this change in custom reflect? there is no clear answer. The region was basic in the great movements of Goths, Vandals and Burgundians under the Later Empire, and, behind these movements, the frontiers of the 2nd century are too indistinct for use. The cultural division extending southwards from the gulf of Danzig roughly along the line of the Passarge river is clear enough archaeologically, but cannot be translated into history.

In the 3rd and 4th centuries the lands flanking the lower Vistula became the repository of certain types of bronze- and glass-ware for which an origin in south-eastern Europe is predicated. These include bronze bowls covered with curved flutings, and certain types of glass beaker of kinds not present in the Rhenish or Belgian factories. More will be said of these wares at a later stage. Meanwhile, it may be observed that their distribution in the Baltic lands is rein-forced by the astonishing concentration hereabouts of gold coins, *solidi*, mostly of the Eastern Empire and of dates ranging from the end of the 4th through the 5th century.

Gold had now replaced silver as the staple currency or treasure, and gold matched the taste of east-European

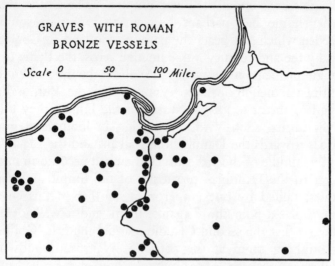

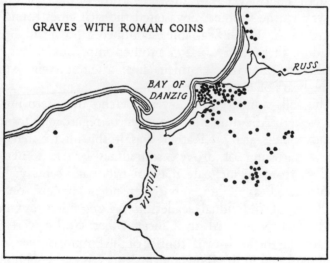

Fig. 2 Differential distribution of Roman bronze vessels and coins. (*After H. J. Eggers*)

barbarism. It lined the Baltic and flowed over into the Swedish islands and the pages of the sagas.

The new emphasis thus attached to a south-north circulation in eastern Europe is consistent with certain familiar
historic trends under the Later Empire. The Goths, whose
earlier home had perhaps been in that part of southern
Sweden which still bears the name of Gotland or Götalund,
had by the 2nd century A.D. extended across the Baltic to the
Danzig plain and its environs. At about the time when their
continental neighbours, the Vandals and the Burgundians,
began to thrust south-westwards to the Rhine, they themselves turned southwards, advancing in loosely integrated
hordes towards the Danube, the Balkans and the Black Sea.
By the middle of the 3rd century they had become an instant
threat to the Danubian territories of the Empire. Roman
armies, rallied by one emperor or another in this chaotic
time, made a poor show against them, and it was not until
A.D. 269 that the second Claudius earned the title 'Gothicus'
by crushing them at the battle of Naissus, far down in
modern Yugoslavia. Meanwhile, a host of them had made
its way to the Crimea, devastated the rich cities round the
shores of the Black Sea, and established a powerful Gothic
kingdom there. In A.D. 276 another emperor, Tacitus, was
earning the same title 'Gothicus' in an attempt to check them
in the heart of Asia Minor.

This folk-wandering over vast stretches of eastern Europe
and western Asia must not, however, be regarded in terms of
an advancing army. Rather was it the intermittent and
partial thrusting of droves, sometimes larger, sometimes
smaller, from an inchoate mass of tribes and septs vaguely
co-ordinated as 'Goths', but dependent largely on the
accidents of individual leadership. Long after a Gothic
horde had penetrated to Cilicia, other Goths were still
threatening the Danubian frontier of the Empire or were even
being enrolled in the Roman army; and, as every schoolboy
knows, in A.D. 410 a Gothic king sacked Rome itself. In the
3rd and 4th centuries, from the Baltic to the Danube and the
Black Sea, in contact alike with Italy and the Eastern Empire,
was a continuum of German peoples who may be loosely

aggregated as Goths: to be complicated but not entirely broken at the end of our period (after A.D. 370) by the first incursions of the Asiatic Huns, whose depredations in and beyond the Danubian regions lie mostly outside the present story. The context was complete for that increasing circulation of Roman, and particularly East Roman, things throughout this wide, uneasy zone and turbulent period. Our bronzes and glassware of non-western types in East Prussia and the Baltic are an acceptable illustration of the process; whilst upwards of 54 hoards of late 2nd or early 3rd century *denarii* in Russia, containing more than 11,000 coins, and at least 17 hoards of similar kind from Poland (over 10,000 coins)[1] probably reflect the same complex of events. Finally, the Runic alphabet which appears to have been evolved in contact with the Greek and Latin alphabets shortly before or after A.D. 200 may have been invented by the Goths[2]; it at least owed its early and widespread distribution between south-eastern Europe and Scandinavia to the constant interchange of commodities and ideas within this Gothic zone.

Jutland and the Baltic Islands. Mention has been made in the preceding section of the abundant gold coinage, mostly of the Eastern Empire, which in and after the end of the 4th century A.D. overflowed to the Prussian coast and the Swedish islands, Gotland and Öland. By the 5th century these islands were in the main stream of a vigorous if superficial intercourse between the Black Sea and the Byzantine world on the one hand and Scandinavia on the other. But in earlier times the hegemony of the Baltic lay rather with the great Danish islands—Zealand, Fyen, Laaland—which bar its outlet towards the Kattegat and the North Sea. These —indeed, all the major Baltic islands—were at the same time sufficiently large, sufficiently secluded, and yet sufficiently accessible to support effective groups of seafarers and their

[1] T. Arne in *Oldtiden*, VII, 208.

[2] Summary of views in H. Shetelig and H. Falk, *Scandinavian Archaeology* (Oxford, 1937), chap. XIII.

families under conditions of security hard to obtain on the mainland. Through-shipping must often have sought them, whether from choice or from adverse winds, and have contributed to their wealth. As bases for trade or piracy they had everything to offer. And their amenities extended to the sounds and firths of the Jutish peninsula, where was also a natural store of exportable amber. It is here then, at the western end of the inland sea, on island and mainland, that our maps show an early and continuing bias towards imported wares. For example, of more than 500 Roman vessels of bronze and 300 of glass known from Scandinavia, a great majority come from Denmark.

Land- and sea-routes, sources in the south-east and in the south-west, alike contributed to this concentration. At one time or another in the first four centuries A.D. Denmark drew its exotic wealth down the Oder and the Elbe from central and southern Europe, and by the North Sea coast from Gaul. The first check came with the great tribal movements which broke the Rhine-Danube frontier of the Empire in A.D. 258-60. Coin-evidence suggests that from that time the Elbe route, hitherto fostered by the Thuringians or Hermunduri beside its middle reaches (p. 22), ceased to play any important part in the business. And though goods from the Roman world continued in one way and another to reach Denmark throughout the 4th century, the main axis thereafter swung eastwards to the Swedish islands and the Pomeranian-East Prussian seaboard, which has been well described as one long quay at this period, busiest at its eastern end about the delta of the Vistula.

The cultural unity and uniform wealth of Jutland and the Danish islands in the first three centuries A.D. is difficult to understand save in terms of some sort of political unity on which history is silent. A West Baltic kingdom with a sphere of influence extending to the mainland on the west and south would explain the attractiveness of this region to North Sea and continental traffic, and would make sense of our distribution-maps (e.g. fig. 8). It is tempting to suppose that something of the old spirit of the Cimbri, who had ravaged western Europe at the end of the 2nd century B.C., survived here in the neighbourhood of their original peninsular home, and possibly derived a new force from the compression imposed by the Imperial frontier. On the other hand, a closer analysis of the Danish evidence has suggested that this inferred West Baltic kingdom may have been centred primarily, not on the Jutish or Cimbric peninsula, but rather on the neighbouring islands, and that it spread thence to the mainland at a relatively late date. About A.D. 200 a break has been observed in the native culture of Jutland.[1] Pottery-types and brooch-forms change about that time, villages are abandoned, cemeteries discontinued. New cultural influences now come in from the islands, where the tradition remains unbroken. The evidence requires further thought, but meanwhile the picture is that of an island-kingdom of the 2nd century A.D., with headquarters perhaps on Zealand, abruptly extending its dominion into the peninsula early in the following century and somewhat drastically remodelling the way of life there. The 3rd century, be it added, was the heyday of the vast peat-bog deposits (p. 54), which, whatever their precise cause, sufficiently show that great things were afoot at that time.

Then in the eastern Baltic we seem to have in the time of the Later Empire a successor state or federation to this western kingdom at a time when Goths from southern Sweden and Burgundians from Bornholm had started upon their continental ventures, incidentally unifying the east Baltic coastlands and islands, and transforming them in effect into a sort of 'Gothic base'. Any more precise definition of the political situation in the two Baltic zones would exceed the evidence, but such at least is the trend of the archaeological distributions.

Norway and Sweden. Save for the Swedish islands (in particular Gotland), Norway and Sweden may be described as the 'poor relations' of Europe in the 1st and 2nd centuries

[1] H. Norling-Christensen in *Acta Archaeologica*, XIV (1943), 138.

A.D.   In contrast to Denmark, their distribution maps are significantly thin until the great continental disturbances of the 3rd and 4th centuries gave a new value to these peripheral regions as refuges and bases.   Not a single silver cup of the type well represented in Denmark and northern Germany found its way across the Baltic.   Of the 'chieftains' burials' which have provided a rich harvest of Roman objects on the mainland, only one poverty-stricken example is known from the Scandinavian peninsula.   Even the almost universal *terra sigillata* is absent there, except for a single example from Gotland (fig. 13).   A trickle of Roman goods penetrated to the Oslo, Stavanger and Trondheim fiords and to the lowlands behind Stockholm, and bronze vessels of the plainest and cheapest type occur there (fig. 9). But only when cut-glass vessels or rilled bronze bowls of the Later Empire, or glass drinking-horns of the 4th-5th centuries, began to circulate did the fringe of Norway—in so far as a resistant geography permitted—attract imports of the better class.   The principal interest of these late distributions is that they reflect a new coastwise liveliness and herald the era of the great North Sea folk-wanderings.

IV · CIRCUMSTANCES OF DISCOVERY

GRAVES, settlement-sites, peat-bogs, undefined deposits have all contributed to the very considerable bulk of Roman material now available from Free Germany. In his recent lists, which exclude coins, brooches and beads, Eggers[1] has catalogued no fewer than 2,257 find-spots, some of which have produced a considerable array of objects. Nevertheless, the limitations of this material are worth a moment's thought at the outset, for its recovery has been subject to many distorting conditions. Thus, Denmark and the Netherlands have been more systematically explored than most other regions, and, in particular, the mass of find-spots along the Dutch coast is due largely to this cause. Large areas, on the other hand, such as Poland, which should produce much, have been underworked. Outside Holland, few native settlements of the time of the Empire have been excavated beyond the *limes* or frontier. Graves, though better-recorded, are very liable to be arbitrary in their representation. Rich burials such as the so-called 'chieftains' graves' probably overweight the areas in which they happen to occur. On the other hand the cremation-burials which represent the normal German rite generally contain few grave-goods. Burial customs in one region may specialize in the deposition of coins, in another that of bronze *situlae*, without any necessarily exact relationship to the respective distributions of those objects amongst the contemporary living. Even in a rich cremation-burial, associated objects may have become unrecognizable through burning. Peat-bog dedications, again, are restricted to the distribution of ancient marshes or meres; moreover their discovery is necessarily more fortuitous than that of burials which, even if not marked by mounds, commonly occur in groups or cemeteries. Finally, in assessing the

[1] See Bibliography, p. 182.

evidence after it has been marshalled, how are we to interpret differences of burial custom?—as indices of social stratifica- tion? of chronology? of tribal distribution? Does a con- tinuous, linear distribution reflect a trade-route, a campaign, a migration? Or is it simply a natural zone of occupation? And what, in any particular instance, is the significance of a blank space on the map? Is it merely an accidental gap in knowledge? If not, what is its probable meaning? These are some of the questions which may fairly be asked—and must often enough remain unanswered.

Burials are by far the most productive source of evidence, and amongst them priority must be given to a remarkable group of inhumations which, in spite of an approximate uniformity, are widely spread in place and time.

(a) *Chieftains' graves of the Lübsow group*, so named from their richness and from the occurrence of five of them at Lübsow, between Stettin and Kolberg in Pomerania. They extend from the upper waters of the Oder in the south-east across the German Plain to Fyen and Danish Slesvig in the north-west, with a solitary poor relation in Norway, at Storedal near Oslo (fig. 3). Their limit towards the west is marked by two examples between the Elbe and the Weser. Of the 32 burials recorded,[1] all save two or three are inhuma- tions. The graves are sometimes covered by a mound, but are generally devoid of surviving surface-indication, and the dead were often, perhaps always, placed in wooden coffins. The wealth of their equipment, and the exotic character of much of it, relegate them to a class by themselves. Roman imports include banqueting services consisting of cups of silver or glass, bronze wine-buckets, dishes, jugs, ladles, strainers and 'saucepans', together with toilet objects such as mirrors and combs; whilst among native products are silver or bronze brooches, ornamented hair-pins, gold finger-rings, silver and bronze buckles and other belt-fittings, gold-filigree beads, bronze knives and shears, dice and gaming-pieces, drinking-horns fitted with silver and bronze, casket-fittings,

[1] Eggers, p. 50.

pottery, and sometimes spurs, but, be it noted, never
weapons. Joints of meat were also placed in the graves,

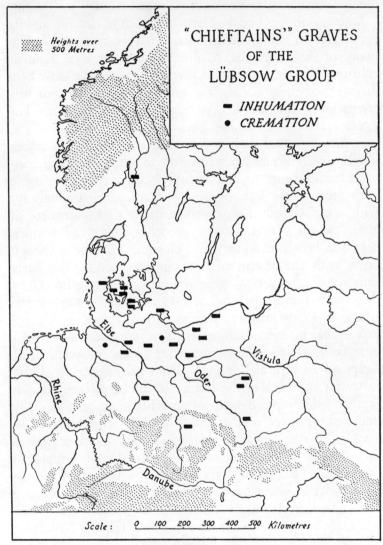

Fig. 3 *(After H. J. Eggers)*

together with a fermented drink made—as traces in the wine-
vessels show—from barley and local berries. ('For drink', says

Tacitus, *Germ.* 23, 'they extract a juice from barley or grain.')
Men and women were buried with equal pomp, as befits
the honourable status ascribed to German women by Tacitus.

Inhumation was not the German Iron Age custom, and its
prevalence in the chieftain-burials has been ascribed, like
many of their contents, to the new contact with Roman
culture. The explanation is invalid, since at the time of a
majority of these burials, the normal Roman custom was
cremation. We are left with a puzzling paradox. For
1,000 years cremation had been the rule in Germany and
Scandinavia. Only when we reach back beyond a rather
shabby and reluctant Early Iron Age to the glorious Scandinavian Early Bronze Age do we find northern rites comparable
with those of the Lübsow group: the dead buried unburnt
with their cherished possessions about them—armlets of
gold, swords, daggers, axes, brooches, skins and textiles,
cups and bowls, even sprigs of blossom. It was as though
now, with the advent of new resources under the Early
Empire, the 'new rich' were reviving the magnificence of
their own remote past. There is nothing to suggest the
arrival of a new aristocracy from without; no known tribal
or national boundary defines the revolutionary mode. An
inter-tribal fashion, based upon an access of wealth, had
swept across central Europe in front of the organized and
masterful approach of the culture of the Mediterranean. It
represented the prerogative of an aristocracy or plutocracy
(merchant princes of the amber trade?) with ideas of its
own—a naïve desire to continue intact in their graves
the delights of a pre-eminently peaceful and sumptuous
existence. That the divergent burial custom, like the intrusive riches, characterized a limited class is in accordance
with analogies from the ancient and modern world. In
India, for example, certain Hindu ruling families have long
inhumed their dead amidst subjects who adhere to cremation.
So about the chieftains' graves of the Lübsow group the
ordinary tribesman normally continued to burn his dead,
humbly enough, in the traditional manner.

This sudden appearance of classical furniture in Free Germany is remarkable, but not without parallel. Much the same sort of thing had indeed happened not very long before within the Celtic fringe some 300 miles further south. In the 5th and 4th centuries B.C. the opening up of eastern Gaul to Mediterranean trade from Massilia (Marseilles) and northern Italy had led to an influx of classical luxuries, particularly wine and table-gear, into the region dominated by wealthy Celtic aristocracies between the Rhine and the Moselle. There had ensued in these parts new standards of good living in what passed for the civilized Mediterranean mode, with all the prestige of 'Etruscan' wine-jars, Greek cups, and bizarre imitations of them. No cultural connection need or can be sought between these Celts and our Lübsow Germans; the common factor is the response of a flamboyant barbarism to sudden opportunity for exotic display and affectation.

By what route or routes the Roman imports reached these Lübsow chieftains is clear enough. Some contact from an early date with the romanized West either by land or by the North Sea cannot be precluded, but there can be no doubt that the principal approach was from Italy direct, by the Danube and the March to the systems of the Elbe and the Oder. The map-distribution and the character of the imports combine in proof, and a third factor coincides. With scarcely an exception, the imports to which a southern (mostly Italian) origin may be ascribed antedate the great war against the Marcomanni and the Quadi of Bohemia in A.D. 167-73 (above, p. 21). This war, and the prolonged disturbances of which it was a peak, must seriously have restricted trans-Alpine traffic; and it can be no mere chance that it was only then and thereafter that the Lübsow 'chieftains' or their successors turned mainly to western markets for their goods, their old sources of supply now largely closed to them.

At the same time, a source of supply other than normal long-distance trade may in some cases be suspected. Diplomatic gifts of plate to ingratiate native princes are attested by Tacitus for Germany (above, p. 10) and by the *Periplus* for the East (below, p. 116), and some of the more costly collections of classical table-ware from Free Germany may have originated in this practice. The nearest approach to direct evidence for it is supplied by the famous find from Hoby, which constitutes the most remarkable assemblage of classical metal-wares from any single spot in Free Germany, with the exception of the Hildesheim hoard and the peat-bog deposits.

In 1920 at Hoby, on the south coast of the Danish island of Laaland, a richly furnished burial was found by chance and excavated without method.[1] The general features are, however, clear. In an unmarked grave lay the skeleton of a middle-aged man with his head towards the north-east. No evidence of a coffin was observed, but on analogy it is not unlikely that one was present. Beside the dead had been buried two joints of pork and a magnificent table-service, mostly in the more northerly part of the grave near the head and chest of the skeleton. The equipment included a pair of decorated classical silver cups placed on a bronze tray which had been tinned internally; a plain silver cup or ladle to which a vigorous zoomorphic handle of bronze had been fitted by a non-classical craftsman; also of bronze, a *situla* or bucket, a *patera* or saucepan, a jug; two bronze-mounted drinking-horns; seven brooches of bronze or silver, one with inlaid gold; two gold finger-rings; a bronze belt-buckle; a bronze knife; a bone pin; and three clay pots. The datable objects are of the end of the 1st century B.C. or the beginning of the 1st century A.D., the time of Augustus. The burial thus constitutes probably the earliest of the known chieftains' graves of the Imperial period.

The two cups at the head of the list are cylindrical two-handled *scyphi* (a handle of one of them missing), and are finely decorated in relief in a style inherited by the academic age of Augustus from Hellenistic sculpture or painting of

[1] K. Friis Johansen, 'Hoby-fundet', in *Nordiska Fortidsminder*, II, Hefte 3.

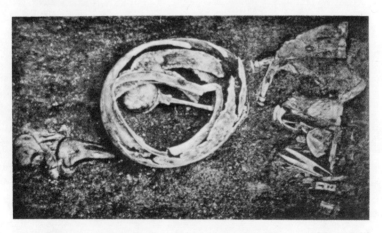

Roman bronze vessels and glass, with drinking-horns, etc., in a 'chieftain's'
grave at Juellinge, Laaland.   (Two portions of the same grave.)
(*See p.* 41)

Roman vessels of bronze (1 and 4) and glass (2 and 3) from 'chieftain's' graves at Juellinge, Laaland.   1 and 4, $\frac{1}{3}$; 2 and 3, $\frac{1}{2}$ (See p. 41)

A. Silver cup, partially gilt, from the 'chieftain's' grave, Lübsow I. ½
(*See p.* 43)

B. Glass cup with silver overlay from Varpelev, Zealand. ⅔
(*See p.* 71)

VI

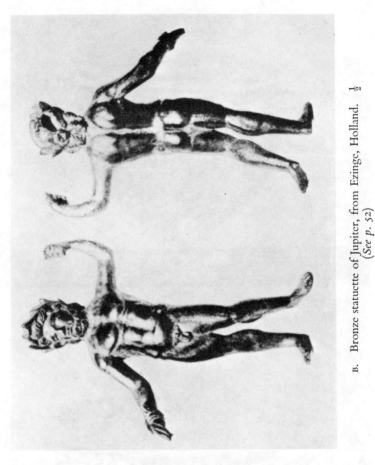

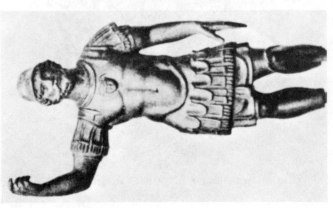

A. Bronze statuette of Mars, from Tybjerggaard, Denmark. ½ (*See p.* 52)

B. Bronze statuette of Jupiter, from Ezinge, Holland. ½ (*See p.* 52)

the 4th century B.C. One represents the visit of Priam to Achilles as recounted in the *Iliad* (pl. IA, p. 20); the other derives its subjects from the legend of Philoctetes and is probably based upon the lost *Philoctetes* of Euripides. In both, certain details of the costume and ornament are gilded. Both are signed in stippled letters by a maker named Cheirisophos, the one in Greek lettering, the other in Roman, though with the Greek form of the name. Cheirisophos was evidently a Greek craftsman, working possibly in Asia Minor, where Pliny places a centre of production, or perhaps rather in Alexandria, with an eye to the Roman market. The Philoctetes cup also bears, as these vessels often do, an indication of the total weight of the pair, and finally a graffito on the base of both gives *Silius* as the name presumably of a former owner. Two comparable *scyphi* are in the great treasure of Bosco Reale, near Pompeii, where also the weights of important pieces and the names of owners are inscribed. The bronze tray on which the Hoby cups stood is of a kind more familiar to-day in the innumerable red-glazed copies made by the Arretine potters. The jug is of exceptional beauty, with a finely wrought frieze of tendril-pattern and a charming little cupid at the base of a high and graceful handle (pl. II, p. 21). The two-handled dish is of comparable workmanship and has a scutcheon ornamented in relief with a figure of Venus decked by cupids. The *situla* has a floriate handle with swan's-head terminals and attachments adorned with cupid-masks. The type has a wide south-east to north-west distribution across central Europe, and even extends occasionally into Norway and Sweden. Its Campanian origin is not in doubt, and its bearers probably brought it via Aquileia and the Danube, though a coastal route from the mouth of the Rhine is possible. To a similar origin in southern Italy may be ascribed the *patera*, which bears the maker's stamp of Cn. Trebellius Romanus. For the rest, the contents of the grave are of non-Roman workmanship. The pair of drinking-horns have knobbed or 'baluster' terminals of the longer

D

and earlier type. Most of the brooches belong to a specifically Danish series of the early Roman period; and, lastly,
the pottery is, as might be expected, also of local provenance.

In grave-deposits, cups and drinking-horns are found,
hospitably enough, in pairs according to an established
Roman habit,[1] though the concurrence of the two types of
vessel—whether for different beverages or customs, or
whether the foreign silver was merely an added luxury—
is not explained. At any rate, Campania and Asia Minor or
Alexandria had contributed lavishly to the gear of the dead
man of Hoby, lying there with his clothing pinned about
him by a fine array of native brooches. The question
remains: How had a complete Roman drinking-service,
consisting of no less than eight pieces, come to this far-off
Danish island and to a single grave? By trade, it may be;
but here if anywhere we have an example of the diplomatic
presentation of gold and silver plate referred to by Tacitus.
For it has been plausibly suggested that the 'Silius' who had
owned the silver cup was none other than the C. Silius who
was legate of Upper Germany from A.D. 14 to 21.

Another burial of the same general kind but a century
later in date shows interesting variations in detail and is better
recorded. At Dollerup, about 10 miles west of Kolding in

---

[1] Represented, for example, in the hoards from Bosco Reale and the House
of Menander at Pompeii, and, far away in pre-Claudian Britain, in the two
imported silver cups at Welwyn, Hertfordshire. Chemical analysis has shown
that, of a pair of native drinking-horns of early Imperial date found in a peat-
bog at Skudstrup, Kr. Hadersleben, in Danish Slesvig, one had contained mead
from honey, the other beer from emmer-wheat. Whether the pairs of classical
cups had similarly contained different kinds of wine or were merely a symbol of
hospitality is not known. The latter explanation seems unlikely. Whatever
the meaning of the custom, it was represented in no less than 17 of the 'chieftains' graves' by pairs of metal or glass drinking-vessels, and had been taken
over from the Roman world with the goods themselves. When the source of
supply shifted from Italy to Gaul in the latter half of the 2nd century, cups were
no longer distributed in pairs; nevertheless, their German recipients continued to observe the Italian custom and made up pairs of odd vessels. See J.
Werner, 'Römische Trinkgefässe in germanischen Gräbern der Kaiserzeit', in
Ur- und Frühgeschichte als historische Wissenschaft (E. Wahle Festschrift), ed. by
H. Kirchner (Heidelberg, 1950), pp. 168-76.

the Ribe district at the base of the Jutland peninsula, the discovery of pottery and other relics of various dates within the Roman period led in 1947 to a methodical exploration which revealed a remarkable double burial.[1] Two graves lay parallel with each other, roughly east and west, with less than 1 m. between them, and the symmetrical but over-lapping disposition of pots upon this intervening balk seemed to indicate simultaneous burial. The bodies had been placed in oak coffins of semicircular section, preserving the contour of the tree, and had been laid out on, or shrouded in, cow-hide. The pattern of the grave-goods showed that the heads had been towards the west, although the actual bones had disappeared save for some of the teeth. The more northerly grave contained a large pottery vase near the head; an iron brooch with silver inlay and traces of cloth where the chest had been, recalling the words of Tacitus (*Germ.* 17) that 'the universal dress is the short cloak, fastened with a brooch or, failing that, a thorn'; two drinking-horns with bronze mouth-rings close to the face of the dead and, at the pointed ends, bronze caps in the form of ox-heads; adjoining these, fragments of silver hooks and bronze fittings, including a buckle; a plain gold finger-ring; two rows of ornamented silver studs; and at the foot two clay vessels—a cup and a dish—with an iron knife and indeterminate objects of iron and wood. The more southerly grave included similarly a large pottery vase near the head; a silver brooch at the base of the throat, with remains of cloth, hide, cord and a bead or pendant of silver wire; two plain gold finger-rings where the right hand had presumably been; towards the foot of the coffin, two prick-spurs of bronze with silver filigree and iron points, and two sets of three round silver filigree discs with pierced lugs for attachment, traces of silver ornaments and a blue glass bead; and, beyond these, an iron knife with remains of a silver-mounted sheath, two bronze *situlae* or buckets which may have been wrapped in cloth, two clay pots, and

[1] O. Voss and M. Ørsnes-Christensen in *Acta Archaeologica*, XIX (Copenhagen, 1948), 209ff.

two silver cups which had stood upon a round wooden tray; and, lastly, fragments of a bone comb. The southern grave had evidently been that of a man, but whether the northern had been that of a woman is less certain.

Typical analysis of this varied assortment of objects, particularly of the *situlae*, brooches, spurs and comb, indicates a date not earlier than the end of the 1st and more probably within the 2nd century A.D. for the two burials. In the present context interest attaches primarily to the bronze buckets and the silver cups. The former, 25·5 cm. high, are of double-conical form (Eggers types 24-9),[1] each with three pelta-shaped feet, a pail-handle, and soldered handle-attachments bearing human masks flanked by fish-heads. Similar handle-attachments were found long ago in a mound at Højsted (Rumperup) in the Holbaek district of Denmark with a *patera* stamped by L. Ansius Epaphroditus, who worked in Campania in the latter half of the 1st century A.D. On the other hand, none of these double-conical *situlae* seems to be recorded from Pompeii, so that their vogue would appear to have been after A.D. 79. An example from the Bosco Reale treasure, lost at that time, is typologically earlier; and a central date about A.D. 100, with wide margins, may be ascribed to the Dollerup vessels, always with the possibility of a long life prior to burial.

The two-handled silver cups found beside them are a more difficult problem (pl. IB, p. 20). They are 7·9 cm. high, have bands of zigzag, herring-bone and other simple linear ornamentation round the upper part of the bowl with a fringe of pendant triangles, and the disc-foot of the cup is decorated with a further band of triangles. The handles are flanked at the top (on the 'thumb-plate') by swans' heads and terminate below in a conventionalized animal head with bulbous muzzle. All the ornamentation, including the top surface of the handles, is gold-plated. The cups are of a familiar classical form of the 1st centuries B.C. and A.D., but details point to provincial workmanship. The crude

[1] See Bibliography, p. 182.

ornamentation both on the thumb-plates and on the body is not of the normal Mediterranean standard, and the free use of emphatic triangular or denticular motifs is indeed a feature of the local pottery from the same burial. Non-Roman features have been observed in other cups of the series (p. 36). Certainly the animal head at the base of the Dollerup handles has nothing to do with Roman art; it is comparable with the terminal heads of armlets, finger-rings and belt-fittings over a wide zone of central Europe, extending from Jutland through north Germany to Poland and lower Austria, with a possible origin in the province of Noricum. Thus rather by a process of elimination than by compelling evidence the Dollerup cups have themselves been attributed to a factory somewhere in that gold-producing Roman province. At least it can be affirmed that, however 'barbarian' some of their characters may be, they are as unlikely at this period to have been a product of Free Germany as of metropolitan Italy. It is sufficient to recall the words of Tacitus: 'Heaven has denied them [the Germans] gold and silver—shall I say in mercy or in wrath?'

Yet a third group of burials, somewhat later in date (perhaps A.D. 150-200), may be described briefly to illustrate the range of these rich deposits. Again in the island of Laaland, at Juellinge, four graves were found in 1909, and three of them were excavated with care.[1] They were oriented north-south, and the dead—all apparently women, young and aged —had been buried in coffins, with the heads towards the north. The graves were sealed by a number of large stones, and with the coffins or in the filling above them were joints of lamb; in one case, the complete forepart of a lamb at one end and the hind-quarters at the other. The best-preserved of the burials, now in the National Museum at Copenhagen, may represent the series (pls. III, p. 36 and IV, pp. 36-7). It was that of a woman who had died in her thirties and had, incidentally, been lamed by a deformity of her right leg. She lay on her right side with legs slightly

[1] Sophus Muller, 'Juellinge-fundet', in *Nordiske Fortidsminder*, II, Hefte 1.

flexed, and had been buried with her ornaments and clothing about her: two gold-headed silver pins in her hair, an S-shaped silver clasp with a gold pendant and two gold beads at her neck, four silver brooches (two of them much worn) on the chest and shoulders, two beads of amber and glass under the right wrist, and a plain gold ring on the ring-finger of the right hand. A mass of material under and about the head probably represented a cushion. And held in the right hand was a bronze wine-strainer in the form of a small bowl pierced as a sieve at the end of a long and slender handle.

Beyond the head were the remains of a wooden box with a bronze lock. It had been buried with the lid open, and contained toilet implements: a bone comb, bronze shears, a bone pin, and an S-shaped bronze knife. Beside the box was a pair of Roman cut-glass beakers, and beside them again the remains of a pair of drinking-horns with mounts of partially silvered bronze. Their knobbed terminals are of the shorter and later variety (compare above, p. 37). Beyond the horns again was a bronze cauldron of a plain, convex-sided classical type (Eggers type 40) relatively common in Free Germany in the 2nd and possibly 3rd centuries A.D. Although it is found also, as here, in wealthy graves, it was essentially the 'poor man's' type, and as such had a wide vogue in the poorer lands of the north, Sweden and Norway. Within the cauldron, but formerly, it seems, on a wooden tray placed over it, lay a bronze ladle into which the strainer held by the dead fits; the two instruments were used together in the process of ladling the drink from the cauldron into the beakers or horns. A deposit in the bottom of the cauldron showed on analysis that this had contained a fermented drink made from barley and fruits of the countryside, and the soot which covered the exterior of the cauldron was presumably the result of the mulling of its contents.

The gentility implied by these Juellinge burial-groups with their classical imports of bronze and glass must be tempered by the observation that it was at best of a somewhat shabby kind. At any rate, by the time that they were buried, the imported bronze vessels were much worn and patched, and the fact that one of them, a *patera*, bears the stamp of L. Ansius Diodorus, who worked probably at Capua both before and after the destruction of Pompeii in A.D. 79, has no close bearing upon the date of deposit. Further, at least one of the glass beakers in the grave which has been described was seemingly damaged and useless at the time of burial. Indeed, the whole aspect of the contents of the graves was that either of a decayed heritage from better times or of an economical selection of worn-out commodities, at least in respect of non-native products. All things considered, the date of the series must be well on in the 2nd century.

Finally, it is only fair to the 'Lübsow group' to make some reference to the first of the burials found in 1908 at Lübsow itself, particularly since, unlike those described above, this may possibly have been a cremation. The discovery was, as often, accidental and the precise facts are uncertain,[1] but it would appear that the remains had been placed in a grave perhaps some 6 ft. in length with paved floor, stone-built sides and a large cover-stone, surmounted by a cairn possibly 5 or 6 ft. high. At one end of the grave were clay urns containing ashes which may or may not have been human, and the lower parts of the side-walls showed evidence of fire, supposedly from contact with hot wood-ash brought from the funeral pyre. But in spite of the seeming intrusion of the normal German rite of cremation, the grave has all the general aspect and equipment of an inhumation-grave of 'chieftain' type. Apart from two drinking-horns, four brooches (one of gold and silver), two silver pins and bronze belt-fittings, the contents included a dozen objects of 1st-century date from the Roman world: two silver cups, two glass bowls, a bronze wine-bucket, jug and dish, two bronze 'saucepans' or ladles, a mirror-plate of white metal, and bronze shears and tweezers. The list closely repeats those already given, and details may mostly be omitted. It will suffice to note that the two-handled silver cups had stood

[1] E. Pernice in *Praehistorische Zeitschrift*, IV (1912), 126ff.

upon the bronze dish, as at Hoby; and that they are of a simple and graceful pedestalled form with analogies at Bosco Reale and Hildesheim, plain save for a narrow band of gilded leaf-ornament below the rim (pl. Va, pp. 36-7). As often, under the base of each cup is scratched its weight. The glass bowls—characteristically a pair, like the silver cups and drinking-horns—are of a familiar 1st-century type with vertical 'pillar mouldings' round the sides, and may well be of Campanian manufacture. The bronze bucket is a fine example of the type with 'face-attachments' for the handle, i.e. with the plate attaching the handle-loops to the rim in the form of a human head: in this instance, a female head with a palmette-ruff and flanking animals' (dogs'?) heads, possibly indicating Scylla. A closely similar bucket is included in the Bosco Reale hoard prior to A.D. 79, and the type is regarded therefore as a Campanian product. It penetrated fairly freely by way of the middle Danube to the Elbe-Oder river-system and so to Denmark, with two outliers in Norway (one of them as far north as the Trondheim fiord) and three in Sweden. The larger of the two 'saucepans' or *paterae* is tinned internally and in part externally, and has an early type of handle with a semicircular piercing flanked by swans' heads (fig. 7). This type is particularly common in Bohemia, which may well have acted as an intermediary towards the north. Like the rest of the imported bronze-work in the grave, the bucket may be ascribed to Capuan or at least to Campanian workshops.

These four examples, from Hoby, Dollerup, Juellinge and Lübsow itself, will suffice to illustrate the remarkable character of the 'chieftains' graves of Lübsow'. The durability of many of their contents, with the patent fact that some of these had obviously been long in use before burial, complicates their chronology, but most of them are safely included in the bracket A.D. 50-150. Their distribution, from Jutland to Poland, is too diffuse to conform with any conceivable political amalgam. At the same time, their astonishing uniformity indicates something more than chance. Their furniture shows us a well-to-do society intertribal in scope and shaped by uniform conventions and aspirations: the possession, above all, of a drinking-service, with cups (and drinking-horns) correctly duplicated in the classical tradition, and with containers, ladles and dishes of the orthodox Italian kind. The wine, indeed, in these northern parts had not always seen the Italian sun; the proud owner of Campanian bronze or glass or Graeco-Roman silver must often enough have prefixed his wassailing with an apology for serving the humble mead and cranberry-juice which had contented his ruder ancestors. Rome, which had imposed a new culture upon the conquered west, had simultaneously imposed a new snobbery upon the unconquered north. These mute, inglorious 'chieftains' and their wives, we may suppose, were not immune from this human frailty. But they have richly contributed to archaeology if not to history.

(b) *Other burials.* It may be admitted that to call the wealthy, placid Lübsow folk 'chieftains' is to conform with an archaeological convention rather than to state an ascertained or even probable fact. Nothing that we know of Teutonic chieftainship would lead us to suppose that a prince of Tacitus's Germania would venture into the hereafter without at least a token armament. It may be that contact with the Roman world had brought into being, during the effective tenure of the neighbouring Roman *limes*, a tolerably settled stratum of native 'new rich' not wholly nor even largely identical with the impulsive military aristocracy of the German tradition. If so, the seeming fact that these 'new rich' faded out when major disturbances began to alter the pattern of Free Germany in the latter part of the 2nd century is easy to understand. A hundred years later, their place was taken in central Germany by other 'chieftains', wealthy indeed, but for the rest of a more traditional kind.

These later 'chieftains' have been studied particularly in the region of the Saale and its tributaries south of Halle and

Leipzig.[1] They were buried north-south in large coffins or wood-lined graves, were mostly men—young to middle-aged—dressed and spurred, with gold finger-rings and silver brooches, Roman *paterae*, bowls and dishes of bronze, native and Roman pottery, Roman glass, and with silver spearheads or arrowheads by their side. Roman coins and the types of spur and brooch indicate dates from the end of the 3rd century to the middle of the 4th.

In these same regions are many other humbler graves, at first cremations, later including inhumations. The suggestion of the evidence as a whole is pretty clearly that of a military aristocracy and their followers within raiding-distance of the shrinking Roman frontiers at a time when central Europe was seething with tribal movement and loot was abundant.

For the rest, little need here be said of the large number of burials, mostly cremations, which have yielded Roman goods in other parts of Free Germany. The bulk of the material of our study is derived from them, and their geographical extent is remarkable. In the north they reach the head of the Trondheim fiord in Norway and the province of Vaasa in Finland. The Danish and Swedish islands and eastern Jutland are full of them. Further south they clutter the environs of the great river-valleys and occur more sparsely between them. Frequently the settlements represented by these burials have not been identified; it may be assumed that mostly they consisted of poor huts, such as those described on p. 49.

A single grave-field of the 3rd century A.D. in Hanover will here serve to illustrate in a general way the whole vast series. At Helzendorf, Kr. Grafshaft Hoya, in that province were found in 1936 a number of cremation-burials which produced a medley of Roman and native craftsmanship,[2] the latter

[1] W. Schulz, 'Die Skelettgräber der spätrömischen Zeit in Mitteldeutschland', in *Mannus-Bibliotek* no. 22 (Leipzig, 1922); and Schulz, *Leuna: ein germanischer Bestattungsplatz der spätrömischen Kaiserzeit* (Deutsche Academie der Wissenschaften zu Berlin, 1953).

[2] *Germania*, XXIII (1939), 168ff.

usefully dated by the former. Most of the graves consisted of a hole in the ground in which a bundle of burnt bones had been placed in a cloth wrapping. A few, however, of larger size (75-100 cm. wide and up to 85 cm. deep) contained Roman bronze vessels with their bases set firmly in the underlying sand. Three of these were simple buckets of the so-called 'Hemmoor' type, a Gaulish or Rhineland product characteristic of the 3rd century (p. 78). In two of them with the ashes were remains of a bone comb, and in one the oxidized metal had preserved traces of a bedding of leaves beneath the bones. Another grave produced a bronze bucket or *situla* with cylindrical neck above a carinated body and with loop-attachments in the form of a woman's head between the fore-parts of fish. This is a late variant of the 'face-*situla*', which occurs freely from Bohemia to Zealand—an exception to the rule that after the middle of the 1st century Bohemia withdraws into the background as a Roman market. Presumably the convenience or attractiveness of these *situlae* as ash-containers led to a circumvention of the normal difficulties of trade. In the Helzendorf example the ashes had been bedded in straw. Yet another of the graves contained a bronze tray with vertical sides and vine-leaf handle-loops, the loops or hooks themselves terminating in panthers' heads. Within the tray were a bone comb and clear traces of the linen bag which had contained the burnt bones, and in the same grave was a hand-made native pot. Other objects from the cemetery included a number of native pots, a gold finger-ring with lapis lazuli intaglio, and a *terra sigillata* beaker of 3rd-century type with barbotine decoration (Ludowici form VMg), probably of Rhenish manufacture.

Within the purlieus of the Roman frontier the native villagers were liable on rare occasions in the 3rd or 4th century to adopt the Late Roman custom of inhumation. Thus at Laisack, north of the upper Danube (Raetian) frontier near Neuburg, was found a flat grave containing a skeleton with three bronze arrow- or lance-heads, a silver buckle and four pots, of which one was a black-glazed

Rhenish beaker of familiar late type, inscribed [RE] PLE ('fill up') in white slip.[1] This beaker may have wandered 200 or 300 miles from its place of manufacture, but the mode and route of its wanderings in this period of Roman withdrawal and spasmodic German advance can only be guessed.

(c) *Settlements.* Any attempt to describe the homesteads or villages of Free Germany would exceed the scope of this book. We are not here concerned with the social and economic life of the German or Scandinavian tribesmen save in so far as is necessary to an understanding of the direct or indirect impact of Roman material culture upon them. The remains of their houses accord with the remarks of Tacitus in that they show a simple architecture of timber partially smeared with clay, without masonry or tiles, and are isolated one from another perhaps partly to minimize the risk of fire. Typical examples from Denmark[2] are about 50 ft. long and 15 ft. broad, with lines of wall-posts supplemented externally by walls of peat or turves, and seemingly with turf-covered or thatched roofs, the construction of which was deliberately simplified by the moderateness of their span. The entrance is in the middle of one of the long sides, and the hearth, of stones covered with clay, is more or less central, but not immediately opposite the door. A stone mortar may lie on the clay floor, and there is a tendency for sherds to accumulate round the margins. Here and there scraps of Roman pottery or metalwork, or a Roman Republican or Imperial coin, occasionally of gold but more usually of silver, may be found, but as preserved the imported material from these simple homesteads is not comparable in quantity or quality with that in the inhumation graves further east. These long houses were intended to accommodate cattle as well as the farmer and his family, the living quarters being commonly up-wind, at the eastern end.

Sometimes the distinctive long-house plan is replaced

[1] *Germania* XVIII (1934), 117ff.

[2] For these, see J. Brøndsted, *Danmarks Oldtid* (Copenhagen, 1940), III, 107ff. and 243ff.

by a smaller type, more nearly square and with only two or three posts on each side. The entrance is still central, and the hearth or hearths are on the major axis. Crofts of this kind were indeed probably normal throughout Free Germany. For example, at Wittislingen in Bavaria, on the banks of the Egau, a southern tributary of the Upper Danube in the old province of Raetia, a Roman building of stone was destroyed (as finds show) during the great invasion of the Alamanni in A.D. 259-60.[1] Sometime later, but within the period of the Roman Empire, German settlers occupied the site and built a group of small huts, each about 12 ft. square with floor sunk 1½ ft. below the surface and with three wall-posts on two opposite sides. The sinking of the floor is incidentally a German habit repeated in Saxon huts both in Holland and in England.

Along the Frisian coast between the mouths of the Rhine and the Elbe, local conditions imposed variations in the layout of the homestead. The land surface hereabouts was liable to flooding, and many of the huts and byres were therefore built on extensive artificial mounds or *terps* heaped up to a height of some 10-20 ft. on the local sandy clay or alluvium. These mounds have not infrequently been absorbed to a great extent by the aggradation of the surrounding plain, but attention has been directed to them from time to time in the Dutch sector by intensive agriculture, and these discoveries have been skilfully exploited and supplemented by a society formed for the purpose under the leadership of Professor A. E. van Giffen.[2] Unfortunately, any distribution-map founded on these researches is partially falsified by the accident that the adjacent stretch in Germany, between the Dutch frontier and the Elbe, where a similar type of ancient occupation may be presumed, has been used in modern times predominantly as pasturage and remains undisturbed and unexplored.

[1] *Germania*, 1952, pp. 287ff.
[2] See reports of the Vereeniging voor Terpenonderzoek from 1918 onwards; and *Germania* XX (1936), 40ff.

The mounds range in date from the pre-Roman Iron Age to the Carolingian period or later, though the known pre-Roman examples are rare. A single notable example will serve to represent the sequence. North-west of Gröningen lie large numbers of the mounds—variously known as *Terp*, *Warf*, *Werft*, *Wurt* or *Wierde*—in the vicinity of existing or former streams on the flat Frisian coastland. The summit of the largest mound is crowned by the parish church of Ezinge, at the head of the little town which covers the gentle south-eastern slope. Towards the north, a considerable sector of the mound was carefully excavated by Dr. van Giffen in 1931-4, and revealed a succession of timber farmsteads ranging in date from about 300 B.C. to A.D. 400 or later. To-day the mound is some 1,500 ft. in diameter and rises at the centre about 17 ft. above the natural soil. This height is due partly to the accumulation of occupation-material (remains of floors and turf-walls, posts and wattle, cattle-dung, general debris) through the centuries, but owes much to a periodical building up of the site by the deliberate addition of clay or dung in order to maintain the superimposed homestead above a flood-level which was itself rising with the gradual aggradation of the surrounding plain. The earliest house (Phase VI) lay in fact on the old natural surface; but it was succeeded by a platform which grew in height and diameter through four subsequent phases of occupation. By the Roman period (Phases II-III) it was $11\frac{1}{2}$ ft. high and about 500 ft. in diameter.

With the exception of the crude square hut-pits which represent the ultimate occupation (Phase I) by intrusive Anglo-Saxons about A.D. 400, the successive homesteads are based throughout upon certain uniform elements. These are of considerable interest in the general history of the house-plan, but cannot be more than referred to here. Briefly, they comprise oblong buildings commonly divided into a 'nave' and two 'aisles' by internal lines of posts, three or more in number on each side. The bays of the aisles are sometimes partitioned into stalls, and may be fronted along the sides of the nave by a low wickerwork rack to carry fodder for the stalled cattle. Where the stalls are absent, a hearth (or two hearths) in the nave indicate human occupation. Sometimes both usages are combined in the same building: stalls and racks towards one end and a hearth towards the other. The whole indicates a simple farming economy of a familiar early medieval type, here going well back into the pre-Roman Iron Age. The buildings range in size from a small combined house and byre 31×23 ft. to a monstrous barn with continuous stalls and no hearth, upwards of 76 ft. long. The

Fig. 4 Reconstruction of Early Iron Age homestead at Ezinge, Holland. (*Germania* XX)

aisles (stalls) are about 5 ft. broad. In some instances there is a hint that the main posts may have curved inwards as crucks. The door was placed as nearly as possible centrally either in the end or in the side, or in both.

Each phase was marked by rebuildings which make it difficult to establish a unitary group at any one moment. The clearest *ensemble* is included in the homestead-plan characterizing Phase V which, though approximately of the 3rd century B.C., must closely have resembled its successors of Roman date. The main element in this *ensemble* is a large byre of the kind described, with an aisled addition to one side and flanked on the other by two smaller-aisled dwellings with hearths, and a third combined byre and dwelling. The whole makes a satisfactory reconstruction (fig. 4).

It may be added that amongst the contents of the Roman levels (Phases II-III) were bronze brooches of the 1st century A.D., sherds of plain and decorated *terra sigillata* of the 2nd century, and a bronze statuette of Jupiter. Roman statuettes may indeed be described as characteristic of the region (pl. VI, p. 37): no fewer than 34 of them, from 28 find-spots, have been found in the provinces of Gröningen, Friesland and, in a minor degree, Drenthe. It has indeed been suggested that their numbers are such as to indicate some sort of 'statuette cult' amongst the Frisian farmers, but if so the statuettes are too various to indicate its trend.

In addition to the statuettes, it has been calculated that the provinces mentioned have produced over 50 finds of *terra sigillata* and 200 coins of the 1st-4th centuries A.D., mostly from *terps*. The calculation is probably an underestimate. But it is scarcely necessary to emphasize that in the Frisian culture there was nothing which can be described as Roman in any significant sense. The Frisians, like the neighbouring Batavians to the south-west, had aided the Romans during the campaigns of Drusus and Germanicus, but revolted in A.D. 25 in consequence of tax-oppression and again in A.D. 69-70, when, once more with the Batavians, they achieved an enduring political independence. They appear, however, to have been an essentially peaceful folk, primarily stock-farmers (sheep and cattle, with some horses and pigs), but with an itch for the sea. They traded along the coast and perhaps via the canal whereby Drusus linked their territory with the Rhine in 12 B.C.; acting as carriers to and from the wealthy markets of Jutland and the Danish islands, and doubtless bartering their livestock. In the 3rd century A.D., if not before, they were transporting cattle up the Rhine.[1]

[1] H. Wilkens in *Hansische Geschichtsblätter*, XIV (1908), 310.

A. Silver parade-helmet from the moss of Thorsbjerg, Denmark. $\frac{1}{5}$
(*See p.* 57)

B. Silver bowl imitating glasswork, from Haagerup, Fyen. $\frac{2}{3}$
(*See p.* 70)

Shirt of mail from the Vimose, Fyen. $\frac{1}{8}$ (*See p. 59*)

Enough has been said to indicate broadly the environment in which Roman goods circulated, to a surprising extent, throughout a great part of Free Germany. Save in so far as Roman weapons and armour influenced the German war-gear (and *vice versa*), the impact of the one culture upon the other was, at any rate at first, of no great significance. The two societies were basically far too disparate for fruitful interaction, and Roman sherds or coins on the trampled floor of a German hut meant no more than did the Arretine dishes which strewed the squalid wigwams of Cunobelin at Colchester. But this contact at least served to show the resurgent German tribesmen of the Middle and Later Empire in what directions lay the rewards of victory, and must to that extent have stimulated and even oriented the earlier phases of their wanderings. The alluring taste for half-understood exotic things has often enough helped to bend the course of history.

(*d*) *Loot*. It cannot be doubted that in the turbulent times of the Later Empire the chronic pillaging of the Roman frontier-zone by Alamanni, Franks and other German tribes or confederacies, to say nothing of free-lance piracy, contributed to the diffusion of Roman goods in Free Germany. In the next section the assemblage of Roman and romanizing material in the peat-bog hoards of Denmark will suggest sources of this kind. Rarely, however, can we expect discriminating evidence as between trade and plunder, and this heading need not therefore detain us long. Two examples will suffice. A bronze *situla* of the 'Hemmoor' type (p. 78) and probably of 3rd-century date was recovered long ago from a barrow at Bjorska in the Vastmanland province of Sweden, some 60 miles N.W. of Stockholm. It had been used ultimately to hold the ashes of the dead, but it bears the inscription APOLLINI GRANNO DONVM AMMILLIVS CONSTANS PRAEF TEMPLI IPSIVS VSLLM ('Dedicated to Apollo Grannus by Ammillius Constans, warden of the temple') and, as temple property, is very unlikely to have been given or traded into native hands. The cult of Apollo Grannus had a special

E

vogue in Raetia, and the distribution of the Hemmoor type
is consistent with an origin in that quarter. The region was
traversed by the Alamanni when they broke through the
limes between the Danube and the Rhine in A.D. 213 and
again in 260, and the *situla* doubtless found its way to its
remote find-spot as loot on some occasion of the kind.
Again, at a much earlier date, in wooded country somewhere between the Ems and the Weser had occurred one of
the greatest disasters that ever befell the arms of Rome:
the utter defeat and massacre of the three legions of Varus in
A.D. 9 by the tribesmen of Arminius. This cataclysm
marked the end of systematic Roman exploitation, political
and commercial, towards the Elbe. But meanwhile the
whole of the vast equipment of a considerable army passed
into German hands; and, though we cannot hope to identify
much of it at this long range, the remarkable concentration
of Augustan gold around the scene of the catastrophe can
scarcely be accidental.[1] It is a fair guess to recognize here
some of the spilled treasury of Varus (fig. 5). On the other
hand, the famous silver dinner service found buried at
Hildesheim near Hanover at a considerable distance from the
nearest Roman settlement may in fact be the campaigning
outfit of a Roman commander, but cannot, as has been
suggested, be ascribed to Varus or Germanicus, at any rate
in its entirety, since, whatever the dates of its component
parts, one of the pieces bears what is almost certainly an
Antonine inscription.

(e) *Peat-bog or moss deposits.* Last but by no means least
are the great assemblages of equipment which have been
found during the past century in the mosses of Denmark.
These mosses represent former meres or inlets of the sea
which have in one way or another become isolated and so
have degenerated first into marshland and then into peat-
bog. Sealed successively by water and peat, objects often
of a perishable kind have been preserved with a completeness
rare in surface deposits, and the routine work of peat-cutters

[1] W. Knapke in *Acta Archaeologica*, XIV (Copenhagen, 1943), 58.

has combined with the vigilance of the Danish authorities to recover great quantities of this submerged material. Its presence in the former meres requires explanation, although any explanation must now in part be theoretical. Certain

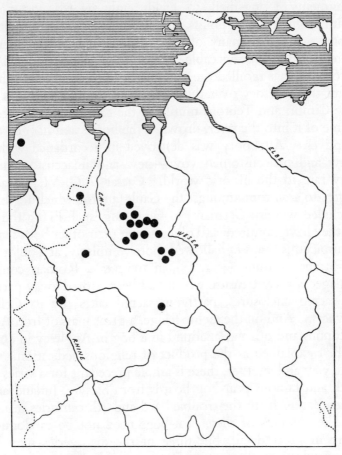

Fig. 5 Distribution of Augustan gold coinage resulting possibly from the Varus disaster, A.D. 9. (*After W. Knapke*)

it is that in Scandinavia from the Stone Age onwards it was customary to dedicate objects of value—large flint axes, flint daggers and saws, bronze axes and swords, bronze trumpets, gold vessels, amber ornaments—by depositing them in the ground, in streams or springs, or in lakes. In the pre-Roman Iron Age this custom was continued and, it seems, given a new turn. Thus at Hjortspring in Danish Slesvig a 30-ft. boat was sunk some time in the 4th or 3rd century B.C. with fragments of ring-mail, 50 shields, eight swords, 170 spears with iron or bone points, and animal carcasses, and it is noteworthy that many of the weapons had been rendered intentionally unserviceable before their deposition. This procedure has recalled the statement of Orosius (V, 16) that, after their victory over the Romans at Orange in 105 B.C., the Cimbri and Teutons mutilated the captured gear, threw some of it into the river, drowned the horses and hanged the captives. 'All booty was destroyed in accordance with a new and unaccustomed vow'—new and unaccustomed at any rate to the historic world. Caesar (B.G. VI, 17) also refers to a custom amongst the Gauls (a term which for him included western Germans) of sacrificing 'such living things as they have captured' and of gathering their other booty into conspicuous heaps in hallowed spots. Similarly, at Toulouse, as Strabo recounts (4. 1. 13), in 106 B.C. a Roman consul pillaged a great treasure which had been 'stored away partly in sacred enclosures, partly in sacred lakes' by its Celtic owners. And on the Celtic fringe, a great mass of Iron Age weapons and other gear found in a bog in Anglesey in 1944 is best explained as the product of religious dedication. In one way and another, there is ample precedent for a series of rich and famous peat-bog hoards from Slesvig, Jutland and Fyen dating from the troubled 3rd and 4th centuries A.D.

The contents of these peat-bogs need not be catalogued here in great detail, but three of the discoveries may be summarized to illustrate their range and character.[1] One of the earliest of them (1858) was that of Thorsbjerg, so-named from the adjacent 'Hill of Thor', a dozen miles north-east of the town of Schleswig, now in Germany, but until 1864 in Denmark. The site is that of a former mere which may anciently have had an outlet to a neighbouring rivulet

[1] See C. Engelhardt, *Denmark in the Early Iron Age* (London, 1866).

and so to the Firth of Sli, three miles to the south. The mere had become a mass of peat 11 ft. thick, and it was in a limited area within the lowest level of this peat, and beneath it, that a remarkable collection of objects was brought to light. A majority of them consisted of arms and armour, but ornaments, tools, agricultural implements and even clothing were included. Exceptional were parts of two Roman parade-helmets: one of thin bronze ornamented with wave- or fire-patterns, a wreathed star and possibly a thunderbolt, the other of silver lined with bronze and partially covered externally with thin gold plates. The latter helmet (pl. VIIA, p. 52) is composed of a face-piece (now lacking a vizor, if it ever had one) and a strapwork crown hinged to it, and is enriched with conventionalized hair and bands of small bosses on the crown and fringing the face. It would be a notable 'find' anywhere, but in this remote spot its interest is enhanced by the mystery of its immediate origin— scarcely an ordinary article of trade, but whether the product of a raid upon the Roman frontier or a diplomatic gift from the Roman world to some native chieftain can only be guessed. Certainly many other objects of Roman provenance were associated with it: fragmentary coats of mail; circular wooden shields,[1] either with round bronze bosses of Roman type—in one instance bearing the dotted name AEL. AELIANVS—or with conical bosses of native type, one with a Runic graffito; the bronze-fitted wooden scabbard of a Roman short-sword, and the wood or metal hilts and fittings of many other swords either of Roman manufacture or native adaptations; javelins (*pila* or angons); brooches, buckles, sandles and other gear. Two discs of gold- and silver-plated bronze incorporate or have been augmented by animals of a semi-Oriental type which the

[1] It may be observed that on Roman monuments, mostly earlier than this hoard, Germans, like Celts, are shown ordinarily with oval or polygonal-oblong shields, and the Hjortspring hoard (above p. 56) includes oblong shields with rounded corners. Circular German-shields occur on the Column of Marcus Aurelius, however, and the round shield was characteristic of the Folk-wandering period. Cf. Tacitus, *Germ.* 43.

Goths spread across Europe from their far-off kingdom by the Black Sea. With all this was a great variety of more specifically native material, though with recurrent romanizing features: iron spears, spear-shafts of ash 8-10 ft. long; long-bows of ash, about 5 ft. long, and iron-shod arrows; whet-stones, horse-harness, parts of wagon- or chariot-wheels, pottery; and five articles of woollen clothing, comprising two cloaks woven in a twill-pattern and in one case green with a yellow and black fringe, a shirt of which the long sleeves are ornamented with a diamond-pattern in the cloth, and two pairs of trousers with loops for the belt and 'feet' of a different and patterned cloth (pl. XIIIA, pp. 84-5). With the great hoard were 37 Roman *denarii* ranging from Nero to Septimius Severus (A.D. 193-211) and sufficiently indicating the 3rd century as a terminal date for the deposit.

About 20 miles north of Thorsbjerg, within three-quarters of a mile of the Als Sound of which it anciently formed an inlet, lies a narrow valley, now floored with peat, the famous moss of Nydam. Beneath the peat, at a depth of 4-7 ft. and covering an area of 10,000 sq. ft., was found in and after 1858 perhaps the most famous of the Danish bog-hoards.[1] Unfortunately, systematic investigation was interrupted by the German invasion of 1864 and, in the words of the Danish investigator, 'the subsequent excavations at that spot, under-taken by German Princes and by a Prussian Baron, do not seem to have been carried on with the necessary care and intelligence'. Nevertheless, a wealth of material had already been recovered, representing much the same range as the Thorsbjerg hoard, but with additions and clearer detail.

The outstanding feature of the Nydam hoard was the presence of three boats, of which one, a clinker-built, sail-less yacht 77 ft. long, was removed almost intact. With the structure of these vessels we are not here concerned; it will suffice to note that they had been pierced and deliberately sunk, and that the objects found in and around them had apparently been on board them at the time of the sinking.

[1] C. Engelhardt, *Nydam Mosefund* (Copenhagen, 1865).

These objects occurred in heaps tied together or wrapped in linen, and included 100 swords, some of them stamped with makers' names in Roman lettering (RICVS, RICCIM, COCILLVS and others); between 500 and 600 heads of javelins and spears; 40 bows and 170 iron arrowheads; a scythe-blade and other tools; dress-fittings and ornaments; and 34 Roman *denarii*, extending from Vitellius to Macrinus (A.D. 217-18). The date of deposition was presumably, therefore, not distant from that of the Thorsbjerg hoard, though the character of certain of the Nydam objects suggests that they may be somewhat later, extending into the 4th century.

A third peat-bog hoard was recovered about the same time from the *Vimose* or Moss of Wi (i.e. temple), near the Firth of Odense in the north-east of the Danish island of Fyen.[1] Of 2,000 objects—swords, one with the stamp TASVIT, sheaths, spears, bows and arrows, a quiver, shields, and much other gear together with wooden bowls and pottery—some special mention may be made of two. One of these is a bronze ornament of Roman workmanship in the form of a griffin's head, probably from a helmet. The other is a complete shirt of mail, the only intact example from Free Germany of a type of armour abundantly represented in the bog-hoards by fragments. The shirt is of bronze-riveted iron rings about ½ in. in diameter, has short sleeves and is about 3½ ft. long, extending to above the knees (pl. VIII, p. 53). Similar shirts of mail are familiar as worn by soldiery on the columns of Trajan and Marcus Aurelius and other Roman monuments, but the type is probably of Asiatic origin and was known to the Germans long before the Imperial period—witness the Hjortspring hoard mentioned above. With the Vimose hoard were coins of Marcus Aurelius and Faustina the Younger, implying a date after A.D. 180, but insufficient for precision.

A review of these hoards and of others like them indicates certain common and significant features. First, they are

[1] C. Engelhardt, *Vimose Fundet* (Copenhagen, 1869).

mostly within easy reach of the sea, and are characteristic of the wealthiest region of Free Germany—namely, the eastern side of the Jutland peninsula and the Danish islands.   Outside this region the only find at all comparable is a later and much simpler one from Kvalsund in Norway.   Secondly, each hoard certainly or probably represents a single deposit rather than a gradual or casual accumulation.   Witness the bundled cargoes of Nydam, with shields in one part, arrows and wooden vessels in another, a group of swords in yet another; or the fact that at Thorsbjerg specific classes of objects were likewise found in separate heaps—for example, several layers of shields pinned together by a javelin which had been thrust through them, or a concentration of gold objects, or of mail, in which spear-heads and small arms might be collected and wrapped.   Thirdly, most of the objects had been deliberately damaged, often not in a fashion which can be ascribed to the incidents of battle.   The shield-bosses are bent and crumpled and broken, a wooden sheath from Thorsbjerg is cut in two and the pieces placed one on the other, many sheaths are deprived of some or all of their mountings, mail shirts are cut and rolled up and the pieces sometimes placed carefully in clay pots, lances are fantastic-ally twisted.   At least one of the Nydam boats had been intentionally and drastically destroyed, and the two boats at Kvalsund had been deliberately shattered so that no two timbers were left fastened together.   More than that, though human skeletons are almost certainly absent from the bog-finds, the bones of slaughtered animals, particularly horses, are abundant, and the butchering has been carried out with an astonishing thoroughness.   Thus a horse's skull from Nydam bears no fewer than 10 sword-cuts, and others show similar treatment.   At the Vimose many horses' skulls and bones were found splintered and hewn to pieces beside chopping-blocks which had been extensively used. Another horse at Nydam had an iron arrowhead in the left shoulder and a second in the ribs.   Detached heads of horses at the same place still had their bits in their mouths.

Equipment and animals alike had been mutilated systematically before being consigned to the mere or inlet in which
the peat has subsequently covered and preserved them.

Two other observations may be added. The hoards, in so
far as they are datable, belong to the period of the Later
Empire, the 3rd or 4th century A.D. And they are linked
predominantly with the Roman world. Many of their
contents were made within the boundaries of the Empire;
many others betray the native craftsman with a knowledge
of Roman things; and, if from time to time a semi-Oriental
element, such as a Scythian-looking animal pattern or
perhaps the bows, may have been derived from south-eastern
Europe, we have to remember that by this time a 'Gothic'
zone extended from the Baltic to the Black Sea and that
from this zone tribal groups—Burgundians, Alamanni and
others—were pushing westwards and familiarizing the West
with south Russian modes.

If now all these various facts are added up, they make a
not unimpressive total. At a number of points readily
accessible to a society based largely upon the sea, great
assemblages of war-gear were sacrificed in a traditional
manner, by slighting and submersion. The picture is, as
we have seen, exactly that painted by Orosius speaking of
the Cimbri and Teutons at Orange, or by Caesar speaking
of the Gauls in general. Whoever the rulers of the Cimbric
peninsula were in the 3rd century A.D., they or their tributary
tribesmen were bringing in to their religious centres great
quantities of loot, mostly obtained either by piracy in the
Baltic or in the English Channel, where the British and
Gaulish shores were now specifically fortified against Saxon
sea-raiders, or, perhaps more probably, from battlefields
somewhere within reasonable range of the Roman frontier.
In the absence of precise dates for the hoards, a closer context
is not feasible. Suffice it to recall that in A.D. 213 the confederation of German tribes known as the Alamanni burst
through the Raetian frontier and heralded a long age of
increasing German pressure on the West. In A.D. 257-8

another confederation, the Franks, from between the Ems and the Rhine, swept through Gaul and into Spain. Two years later the Alamanni were again on the move; they carried destruction across the *limes* into Gaul and, though they were turned by Postumus as 'Emperor of the Gauls', the old frontier territory east of the upper Rhine was never again reoccupied by the Romans in force. Here are a few of many occasions when in the 3rd century Free Germans could have brought home great quantities of frontier loot to their gods in their northern meres, just as in earlier times the Romans had brought German booty home to their Capitol. It may be added that there is some archaeological evidence for the abrupt extension of the native culture of the Danish islands to the Jutland peninsula about A.D. 200 (above, p. 29). But it is no more compulsory to postulate that the bog-finds of Denmark represent great battles fought in Slesvig or on Fyen than that the Roman triumphs of a Germanicus or a Domitian imply victories in the Forum Romanum. Whatever their precise and immediate origin, the general significance of the peat-bog hoards is plain enough as a picturesque footnote to 3rd- and 4th-century history.

V · FREE GERMANY: THE IMPORTS

IN this section selected groups of Roman imports into Free Germany are discussed summarily in respect of date and distribution. No attempt is made to cover the whole field; the maps and lists prepared by Dr. H. J. Eggers in 1951[1] have made any such attempt unnecessary for some time to come. But samples of the coin-finds, metal-wares and glass will serve to illustrate and amplify some of the data collected in the previous sections, and will demonstrate the richness of the field. We begin with a general indication of the evidence of the coins.

a. COINS[2]

Between the Rhine frontier and Latvia, between the Danube and Gotland, some thousands of Roman coins— gold, silver and 'copper'—found their way into the soil of Free Germany and Scandinavia from the time of Augustus onwards. The circumstances of their finding and the significance of their distribution have been discussed by a number of scholars, notably by S. Bolin, whose conclusions hold the field.[3] His detailed analyses are not here recounted, but some of the more general aspects are necessary to our picture, and are in fact implicit in certain of the previous sections.

The coins occur singly and in hoards; of the latter more than 400 are known, and not a few of the single coins may in fact represent ill-recorded hoards. They are found in graves, on settlement-sites, in peat-bogs, and at unrelated find-spots. The extent nevertheless to which they circulated as actual currency amongst the tribesmen was doubtless

---

[1] See Bibliography, p. 182.   [2] Pl. IX, p. 68, and fig. 6.
[3] *Fyndan av romerska mynt i det fria Germanien* (Lund, 1926); résumé in *Bericht der Deutsches Arch. Inst.* 1929 (Frankfort, 1930), 86ff.

relatively slight. When we come to consider the Roman coinage of India, the probability will emerge that there the imported gold and silver coins were used largely in bulk, as bullion guaranteed in quality and perhaps weight by the imperial stamp, but rarely distributed as currency: a supposition reinforced by the absence there of Roman 'copper' coins before the 4th century, and by the deliberate mutilation of Roman gold. The likelihood of a similar attitude in inner Germany is supported by the statement of Tacitus (*Germ.* 5) that 'the Germans nearest to us value gold and silver for their use in trade. . . . The peoples of the interior employ barter.' Consistently with this, in the time of Tacitus, at the end of the 1st century A.D., copper coinage was rare in Germany.[1] Later, on the other hand, presumably as a result of commercial experience, this coinage flowed more freely, and before the end of the Antonine period (2nd century) was not infrequently included in graves as far afield as East Prussia. After this time, copper must have been used fairly widely as 'small change' in the normal processes of monetary circulation, doubtless encouraged by the fact that, with the deterioration of the silver after Trajan and particularly after Septimius Severus, there was an increasing approximation in metal-value between the two categories.

That the quality of the Roman silver was carefully watched by the German traders is clear from the further statement of Tacitus that the Germans preferred 'money that is old and familiar, *denarii* with the notched edge and the type of the two-horse chariot' (pl. IX, p. 68). The barbarian habit of adhering to certain well-known types of foreign coinage is familiar enough, an example being the retention of Maria Theresa dollars in modern Abyssinia. Even the Athenians of the 5th century B.C. found it politic to retain their archaic coin-dies, and Celtic moneyers of the 1st centuries B.C.-A.D. adhered largely to a Macedonian type of the 4th century

[1] Only 36 stray copper coins are recorded from West Germany and Holland (outside the Roman frontier) of dates prior to the end of the 1st century A.D.

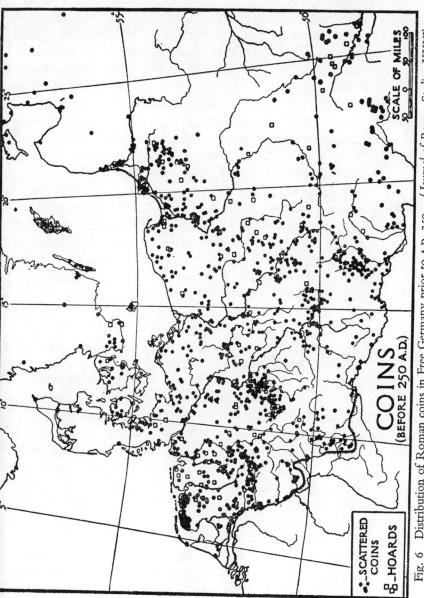

Fig. 6 Distribution of Roman coins in Free Germany prior to A.D. 250. (*Journal of Roman Studies*, XXVI)

B.C. But the conservatism of Tacitus's Germans was not unreasoned; for in A.D. 63 Nero had reduced the silver-content of the denarius and so enhanced the popularity of previous issues in remote markets where intrinsic worth rather than state guarantee was the basis of confidence. Later, a similar ponding-back of pre-Severan denarii seems to have occurred in the 3rd century after the further devaluation of the currency by Septimius Severus. It may be doubted, however, whether the imported coinage ever entered significantly, even as bullion, into the domestic trade of Free Germany; rather may we suspect that its primary use to the German was as a medium for the purchase of other imports from Roman or sub-Roman merchants, of whose penetration into unconquered territories there are many examples. In favour of this supposition is the scarcity of pre-Neronic silver in German hoards later than A.D. 107 when Trajan finally called it in. Most of it must already— or soon afterwards—have found its way back across the Roman frontier.[1]

In summary, then, it is to be supposed that in the peripheral trade of Free Germany, where contact with traders from the Roman world was recurrent, Roman coins circulated in so far as their metal-value was intrinsically acceptable; in the interior and the outlands they were used variously in bulk as bullion, or individually as curiosities, gifts, ornaments, and sometimes as funerary equipment; rarely as a local instrument of exchange, since the Germans, unlike the Celts, were unfamiliar with a monetary system and cannot readily or widely have adopted this alien usage.

Roman gold coinage was unpopular in Germany prior to the 4th century. Its value was presumably too high for normal use. Tacitus (*Germ.* 5) observes that the Germans of the interior tried to get silver in preference to gold; only those 'nearest us' valued both gold and silver. The archaeological evidence confirms the statement. Reference has been made (p. 54) to the scatter of Augustan gold within

[1] Or, as pure silver, into the melting-pot.

range of the Varus disaster of A.D. 9. Apart from this, a small hoard of six aurei of Tiberius, Claudius and Nero has been found at Tensfelderau, Kr. Segeberg, in Schleswig-Holstein; and another of Tiberius is recorded from West Germany. This modest total may be compared with upwards of 13 1st-century hoards of *denarii* in the same region. A hoard of *aurei* of the same date from Bohemia fits in with the historical relationship between the Marcomanni and the empire at this period. Other stray finds of *aurei* from West Germany and Holland of dates prior to A.D. 100 all lie sufficiently near the frontier to require no other explanation.

To the 2nd century A.D. no gold hoards are ascribed, although occasional gold coins of that century, usually pierced or otherwise adapted for ornament, penetrated to Thuringia and Bavaria. Gold of the 3rd century in Germany or Denmark was deposited mostly in the 4th century, when Constantinian *solidi* took the field and were continued by an increasing succession of gold deposits into the 5th century, particularly in Eastern Germany. There the fluid tribal situation—particularly the Gothic and Hunnish migrations —had set up a new current of intercourse between the Baltic and the Black Sea, and new if superficial standards of luxury were emerging under the influence of forceful contact with the Byzantine world.

The distributions of Roman coinage in Free Germany have already constituted a major basis for the section dealing with routes and markets (pp. 11ff.) and, save by maps (figs. 1 and 6), need not be amplified in detail for the general picture which is the purpose of this book. It will suffice to add that under the steadying influence of firm Imperial rule hoards, the non-recovery of which is a sure symptom of a time of trouble, are of rare occurrence in the earlier half of the 2nd century; they do not again become emphatic until the long period of disturbance which began with the Marcomannic war of Marcus Aurelius in A.D. 167. That war was itself merely a focus of unrest extending far beyond the limits of Bohemia. For example, of hoards ending with coins of Marcus Aurelius, five are known from western Germany, three from the mouth of the Vistula, others from Posen, Schleswig-Holstein and Sweden. The Vistula hoards, added to those of Commodus from the same region, may represent a reaction to the earlier movements of the Goths from their Swedish homeland on their long march towards south-eastern Europe (p. 26). But the equation of particular coin-groups with inchoate historical phases of this kind is liable to be an arbitrary business and cannot be stressed. So again a further suggestion, that a series of 3rd-century silver hoards and gold coins, extending down to the emperor Probus (A.D. 276-82), marks the migration of Burgundians and Vandals from east-central Europe towards Gaul about A.D. 278, is of questionable value. It is in fact possible to isolate a number of these finds in an appropriate belt across Germany through southern Brandenburg, Saxony and Thuringia, but only by applying the blind eye to wide variations in dating and distribution. Certainly without the historical background no comparable movement could fairly have been deduced from the coin-evidence as it stands. On the whole, in so confused and turbulent a territory as Free Germany it is best to restrict the use of coins primarily to the analysis of main routes and concentrations, as an amplification of other archaeological evidence, and above all as a chronological control.

b. VESSELS OF SILVER AND GOLD

Free Germany has yielded an impressive quantity of Roman silver-ware, the combined product doubtless of commerce, warfare and diplomacy. Pride of place must be given to the great hoard discovered in 1868 at Hildesheim, south of Hanover, where it had been carefully hidden in a pit about 4 x 3 ft. dug to a depth of some 5 ft. below the former level. Including fragments, it comprised about 70 pieces, and is one of the most remarkable collections of silver known from the ancient world (pls. X-XII, pp.

Early Roman silver coins from Denmark
(See pp. 8 and 64)

69, 84-5). Most of the pieces must have been made within the century 50 B.C.-A.D. 50 with a bias towards the early Augustan period, but the name, Marcus Aurelius, stippled on the base of one of them suggests, without absolute proof, that they were not buried before the name came into prominence in the 2nd century A.D. In the circumstances, guesses as to the conditions of burial are unprofitable. No relevant military or civil site has been identified in the vicinity.

Amongst the contents of the hoard[1] were half a dozen dishes, eight plates and trays, eight bowls, nine cups, two urns, a bucket, four *paterae*, two tripod-tables and a candelabrum, all of silver, sometimes partially gilt: but whether the total represented the luxury equipment of a general officer's 'mess' or whether it was otherwise assembled cannot be deduced with any approach to certainty. It is not merely in quantity that the hoard is outstanding, for two at least of the pieces are unsurpassed amongst the surviving examples of the Graeco-Roman silversmith's craft. One of these is a two-handled dish, elaborately ornamented with honeysuckle and lotus patterns and with a seated figure of Athena set as a central *emblema* in high relief (pl. X, p. 69). Except for the arms, face and neck, the figure is (or was) gilded, and certain elements in the floral design are also picked out with gilding. The quality of the modelling, particularly in the studied but not unrealistic grace of the drapery, reflects the living tradition of Hellenistic sculpture and gives the figure an independent value as a work of art. Where it was made is disputable: Asia Minor and Alexandria are two obvious competitors: but the artist was certainly a Greek.

The other outstanding vessel is a dish with a central relief or *emblema* representing the infant Hercules grasping two snakes, framed by a tendril-pattern issuing from the tails of two griffins and interspersed with birds (pl. XI, p. 84). The pattern, the child's clothing and the snakes were gilded.

[1] E. Pernice and F. Winter, *Der Hildesheimer Silberfund* (Berlin, 1901).

F

There is evidence that the *emblema* is an insertion, and the contrast of its skilled workmanship with the relative coarseness of the tendril adds proof that the two parts did not originally belong to the same vessel. The naturalistic child's head, rendered in the round, is a good example of late Hellenistic genre, in contrast with the more academic Athena of the dish described above.

Other pieces in this famous collection must here be passed by with scarcely a mention: the dishes with *emblemata* representing Attis and Cybele, bowls with the elaborate, naturalistic floral patterns which delighted the Augustan taste, urns with satyrs' masks, herms and theatrical grotesques. Three or four of the pieces show a coarser, less academic handling which has suggested the possibility of a provincial origin for them. Such are an oblong tray (pl. XII, pp. 84-5) with vigorous representations of duck rising from the water or diving below it, and, above all, two conical cups with bold if somewhat uncouth friezes of animals, rosettes and leaf-patterns. These may date from a time nearer that of the burial of the hoard, and may be additions to it from a Gaulish source. Unhappily, surviving examples of Gaulish craftsmanship of the kind are too rare to offer satisfactory proof of this attribution.

If we turn from the Hildesheim hoard to other finds of silverware, we are at once on familiar ground; for of eleven sites which have produced such ware, no fewer than nine are those of 'chieftains' graves' of the Lübsow group. The *scyphi* of Hoby on the island of Laaland, of Dollerup in Jutland, and of Lübsow I in Pomerania have already been described (pp. 36ff.), and, with the exception of a minor cup from Hoby, attributed to a Mediterranean (Graeco-Roman) origin. Others may be ascribed rather to provincial workshops. A pair of plain but graceful cups from a grave at Byrsted in Jutland has been regarded, without certainty or perhaps probability, as Gaulish; but it is likely enough that small silver bowls of late Roman date, vaguely imitating cut-glass vessels, on the one hand from Haagerup in Fyen,

Nordrup in Zealand and Leuna in Saxony, and on the other hand from Chaoucre, Dep. Aisne, were made in Gaul (pl. VIIB, p. 52. A provincial origin has been proposed for the silver cups from Dollerup in Jutland (p. 40); and others from Mollerup, also in Jutland, from the second grave at Lübsow in Pomerania, from Leg Piekarski in Poland and from Holubic near Prague[1] all show un-Roman features, but have not been satisfactorily identified with specific provincial schools. Their normally excellent manufacture, the recurrent use of gilding to emphasize the pattern, and their generally classical types may be taken to indicate origins within the Empire. There is at present no clear hint of any production of this kind and quality within Free Germany itself. It may be added that, with the exception of the bowls from Haagerup, most of the silver vessels from Free Germany belong by type and association to the first two centuries of the Empire, with emphasis on the 1st century rather than the 2nd. In other words, they largely precede the full development of Romano-Gallic craftsmanship.

The region of the Black Sea remains at present an unknown quantity in the luxury trade beyond the frontiers. It may be conjectured that from or through this region came to Varpelev in Zealand an elaborate cup of blue glass with frame and pierced foliage-overlay of silver, incorporating the Greek greeting ΕΥΤΥΧѠΣ (pl. VB, pp. 36-7). With the cup was a coin of Probus (A.D. 276-82), and the burial may not in fact be earlier than the 4th century, but we may recall that from the latter part of the 3rd century south Russia was linked by a more or less continuous Gothic zone with central Europe and the Baltic (p. 26).[2] A similar south-eastern origin has been ascribed to the silver goblets from a well-known find at Valløby in Zealand. The decoration of these goblets, in particular a frieze of backward-looking animals below the

[1] For these cups, see especially O. Voss in *Acta Arch.* XIX (1948), 252ff.

[2] A 2nd-century date and an Italian origin have been ascribed to this cup, and the occurrence of an heirloom in a late grave is not impossible. But I see no reason why the cup should not be of the 3rd century, and the Eastern Mediterranean is a more probable source than Italy.

rim, is consistent with a South Russian origin, and the Goths may again be suspected as the carriers. Against this supposition is the fact that amongst the associated objects was a *sigillata* bowl signed by the potter Comitialis, who worked at Rheinzabern in western Germany during the latter half of the 2nd century, and this date, if accepted literally, is earlier than that of the Gothic kingdom by the Black Sea. Transit up the Danube valley and thence north-wards along one or other of the well-trodden trade-routes from Carnuntum is an alternative possibility which would reconcile date and probable origin without involving the Goths; and a similar path, at any rate from Carnuntum onwards, may have been taken by an attractive silver cup, of low cylindrical form with relief ornament representing masks and a griffin bringing down a stag, found at Ostropa-taka in Czechoslovakia. This cup is, however, of late date and may equally well have passed through Gothic hands beyond the frontier.

The only recorded gold vessel of classical type is a plain chalice, about 6½ in. high, found at Ostropataka with the silver cup just mentioned, and presumably of similar origin and date. The two famous golden drinking-horns from Gallehus in Sleswig,[1] though possibly of late Roman date, have nothing to do with Roman craftsmanship or usage.

C. BRONZE WARE

Of bronze vessels, more than 850 have been found in Free Germany (with Scandinavia), about half of them in Jutland and the Baltic islands. The total is impressive, particularly when it be recalled that sites other than graves have scarcely contributed to it. Apart from the fact that relatively few settlements of the period have been explored, the chance of survival of a metal vessel on an occupation-site is very much less than in a grave. At the same time, it is not to be

---

[1] Conveniently accessible in H. Shetelig and H. Falk, *Scandinavian Archaeo-logy* (Oxford, 1937), p. 208 and Pl. 36.

assumed that the custom of burying these vessels with the dead was coextensive with their total distribution. An examination of the burials in the vicinity of the gulf of Danzig has already demonstrated the contrary (p. 24).

Selected examples must here suffice to illustrate this great mass of material. The series begins, so far as we are concerned, with a number of imports dating from the end of the 1st century B.C. and the first decade of the 1st century A.D., and may here be represented by two distinctive types: a *situla* or wine-bucket with a pair of confronted dolphins at the base of the handle-strap, and a saucepan or casserole with a swan's head on each side of the pierced end of the handle (fig. 7). Of the former, six or seven examples of this period are recorded: four or five from Bohemia and the Thuringian border, one from the Oder valley in Brandenburg, one from Mecklenburg near the Elbe, and one from Hoby in Zealand—all with a single exception from cremation-burials. Predecessors of the same general type had found their way in the 1st century B.C. into the river-valleys of the North German plain as far eastwards as the Vistula and the Passarge, and one had even ventured as far north as Sweden. Their ultimate origin was doubtless in Italy, where Capua dominates the archaeological scene, but whether at this early date they travelled northwards from the Danube or found their way more circuitously through the Celtic lands is not at present clear. The pattern becomes unmistakable, however, in the first decade A.D. The concentration of late Augustan types in Bohemia reflects the régime of the romanizing Marcomannian king Maroboduus and the recorded activity of Roman traders amongst his tribesmen (p. 19). The old Aquileia-Danube route was now systematized via Carnuntum in the methodical Augustan manner, and a reasonably regular traffic along it was the natural sequel. Dolphin-buckets and swan-saucepans travelled that way, and no fewer than twenty of the latter have been recovered from Marcomannian graves, with an outlier near the valley of the lower March as a pointer.

Further north, the swan-saucepans reached the valleys of the
Oder and the Weser, but only one of them made Scandinavia
—a strangely isolated example from a grave at Kvåle, far
up the Sogne fiord 80 miles north-east of Bergen.   Only

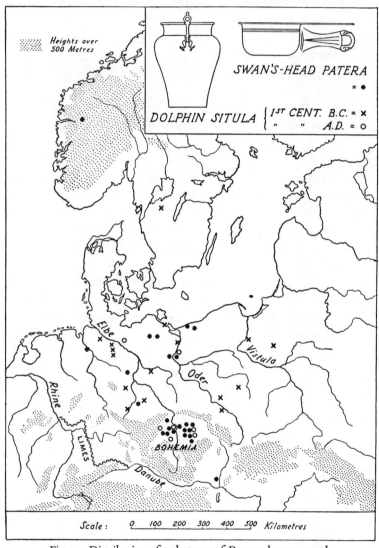

Fig. 7   Distribution of early types of Roman bronze vessels
(*After H. J. Eggers*)

two of them approached the Baltic coast, and there is no reason for associating the distribution of either type specifically within the amber trade.

Other early Imperial types confirm these distributions: for example, buckets or *situlae* with a human mask on the attachments of the handle-loops such as that already described from Lübsow (p. 44), *paterae* with ram's-head handles, and round-bottomed ladles or strainers with oar-shaped handles, the bowls of the strainers pierced at first in the form of a maeander. These imports extend the map-pattern slightly towards Poland and Sweden, but the main bulk of them remains concentrated in central Europe and Denmark. Italy —in particular, Campania—was still the source of supply, and the Carnuntum route remained the principal approach. As the 1st century wore on, however, a variation began to emerge: after the flight of Maroboduus in A.D. 18 (p. 21), Bohemia, home of the Marcomanni, gradually lost the commercial impetus which the king had given to it, and was increasingly by-passed by the Italian trade with the north. An illustration will make this clear. Partially contemporary with the swan-handled saucepans already mentioned, but outlasting them, were other types marked by a swan-less half-round or circular piercing through the handle. These scarcely occur in Bohemia, but are abundant further north, particularly in the Danish islands. Eggers notes that, of those with the circular piercing, only two have been recorded from Bohemia as against no fewer than 51 from Denmark, mostly from inhumation-graves (fig. 8). The map-pattern, now focused on *c.* A.D. 50 and later, still suggests a Danubian rather than a Gaulish or North Sea approach, but against this must be set the cessation of the productive graves towards the west. In the circumstances, it is, as often, impossible, in the interpretation of the map, to estimate the extent to which the distribution of a burial custom may distort the archaeological distribution. One other early type calls for remark even in a summary list. This is a plain convex-sided bronze pail about 9 in. high, with simple eyelet for the handle, known as the 'Eastland' type. Ten of these occur in the territory of the Marcomanni, whom they presumably reached in the first quarter of the 1st century A.D. For the rest, they cover what we may now term the conventional early 1st-century

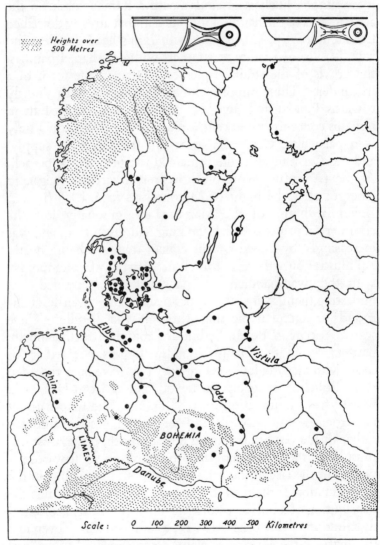

Fig. 8 Distribution of Roman *paterae* with circular-piercing
(*After H. J. Eggers*)

zone in central Europe and Denmark; but the type lasted on well into the 2nd century and perhaps even later (p. 42), and, unlike the contemporary types already discussed, spread across into Norway and Sweden, where, excluding the

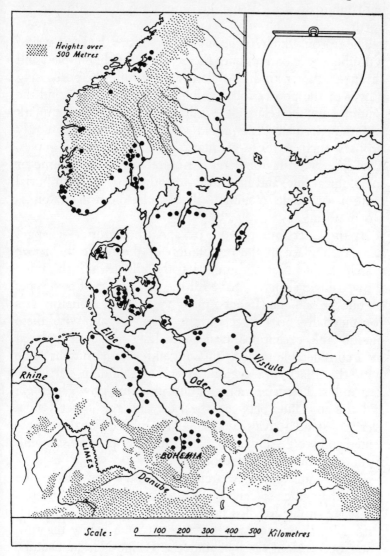

Fig. 9 Distribution of 'the poor-man's bucket.' *(After H. J. Eggers)*

Swedish islands, over 50 examples have been found (fig. 9.) In Norway they are probably all derived from cremation-graves, in which they conveniently contained the ashes. In Sweden they occasionally occur also as grave-furniture with inhumations. Why this unusual spread into the far north?

The reason which has been given by more than one writer is doubtless the correct one: these vessels are the simplest and cheapest of their kind, and were alone within the purchasing power of the poorer folk of the hills and fiords beyond the Baltic; only the relatively wealthy aristocracy of Denmark and the German Plain could afford elaborate and costly bronzes such as those of many of the chieftains' graves. The differential factor here, therefore, was an economic or sociological one, and had little or nothing to do with burial custom or trade facilities. The archaeological lesson is worth noting.

By the Later Empire—the 3rd and 4th centuries—changes had taken place in the orientation of the traffic in bronze vessels, as of other commodities, though in bulk the trade showed little change. Save for the occurrence of two types of bucket or *situla* (Eggers, maps 17 and 20), Bohemia was commercially no longer on the map. Again with these questionable exceptions, trade with Italy had been replaced by a considerable trade with Gaul and an intermittent trade with the Black Sea region. Denmark, and in particular Zealand, still remained a major customer, but now Thuringia and the lowlands between the Elbe and the lower Rhine were substantial rivals, whilst Poland is occasionally represented and would doubtless make a more impressive showing if more adequately explored.

To illustrate these new trends, no better example can be taken than the so-called 'Hemmoor' buckets (fig. 10). These are simple handled bowls 7-9 ins. high on a footstand, with a linear or, occasionally, figured zone below the rim. They occur along and behind the Rhine-Neckar-Danube frontier, not infrequently in hoards, which have been

associated with the break-through of the Alamanni in these
parts about A.D. 258.   Their Gaulish or West German origin

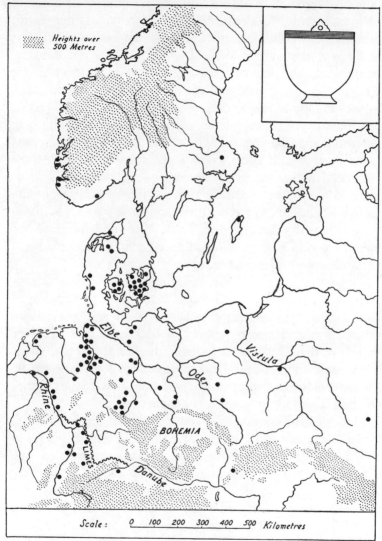

Fig. 10   Distribution of 'Hemmoor' buckets.   (*After H. J. Eggers*)

is certain, and their manufacture has been variously ascribed
to Cologne and to the neighbourhood of Aachen; an

inscribed example from as far afield as Sweden may have come from Raetia (p. 53). An analysis of their distribution beyond the frontier suggests interesting interpretations. In Denmark and Mecklenburg they are found largely with inhumation-burials, and the same rule applies to Thuringia; in Lausitz they are associated with, but do not contain, cremations, and are often 'ritually broken' in accordance with a widespread funeral custom. From the mouth of the Elbe to the lower Rhine they occur also in cremation-graves, but here as containers of the burnt bones. How far these variations may be equated with tribal groups is a dangerous speculation which must await some future analysis of the associated native cultures. In any event, the task is complicated almost beyond hope by the fluid condition of the German tribes in the 3rd century; and to suggest, as has been done, that the Lausitz folk were Burgundians and the western group Saxons is to outpace both the historical and the archaeological evidence.

These vessels, and others of the same phase—straight-sided bronze basins, late bronze strainers with oar-shaped handle and flat base (Eggers types 78-88 and 161), were doubtless distributed by the standard routes: the tributary valleys of the Rhine as far south as the Main, and the North Sea coast extended by a land-traverse across the base of the Jutland peninsula. It is worthy of note that five examples reached the southern coast of Norway.

Mention of Norway may remind us that, except for the islands, Norway and Sweden have mostly been peripheral to our study. Now, however, in the 4th century, on one occasion they dominate the scene. A group of bucket-handled bronze vessels with cylindrical neck and sharply rounded or carinated body (Eggers types 11-14, 'Westland type') occurs in 19 cremation-burials in Norway and Sweden, reaching as far north as the Trondheim fiord on the west and Sundsvall on the east; the latter point may have been reached by a land-route across country from the former (fig. 11). This remarkable distribution is emphasized by the fact that only four examples are known from Free Germany south of the Baltic—one each from inhumation-burials on Fyen and in Mecklenburg, one from a cremation at the mouth of the Elbe, and one from a peat deposit by the middle

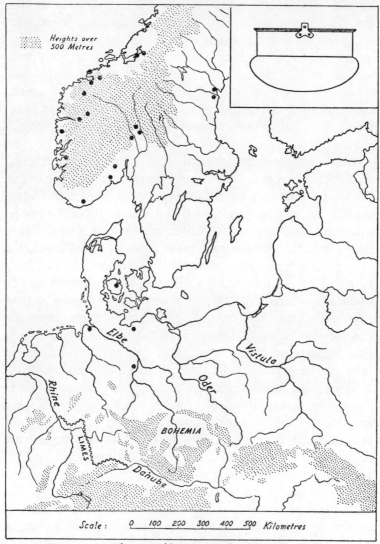

Fig. 11 Distribution of bronze vessels of 'Westland' type
(*After H. J. Eggers*)

reaches of the river. Owing to the general absence of associated goods from the northern graves, the chronology of these vessels is largely theoretical, though the late Roman dating is fairly well established by the two inhumation-burials. They are later, perhaps considerably later, than the 'Hemmoor' type, and may well, as Eggers suggests, spill over into the 5th century. A similar suspicion arises in regard to other late groups of bronze or glass with a comparable though less isolated distribution (p. 30). If so, they are a not undramatic expression of coastal concentration and activity on the eve of the great Folk-wandering. But the evidence is at present of a sketchy character.

Traffic with southern or south-eastern Europe, in particular the Black Sea region, has already been illustrated tentatively (p. 24) by reference to certain types of fluted bronze vessel which, rather by process of elimination than by direct evidence, have been ascribed alternatively to that source or to Italy (fig. 12). Of the two main types of fluted bowl, the earlier, which seems to emerge a little before A.D. 200, has a rounded profile, fine fluting and a twisted handle with attachment-loops flanked by swans' heads. The type-site is Gile, near Oslo, and the type is, curiously enough, relatively common in Norway, though it also occurs on eight sites in East Prussia and Pomerania. The later variety has upright sides, coarser fluting and a plain handle, and is known as the Valløby type from a site in Zealand. This also appears in the lands beside the lower Vistula. Along the Gaulish frontier the general type occurs rarely and only in circumstances which can be explained by garrison-movement from central or eastern Europe. In Italy the type is not known, but our knowledge there of post-Pompeiian metalwork is slight. It may occur on the margins of the Black Sea, but these are at present barred to research. The most certain and significant feature attending it is its presence in some force in East Prussia, northern Poland and eastern Pomerania, a region approached from the south-east by the river-arteries of the Vistula and the Dniester; and Italy is perhaps less likely as the starting-point than are the obscured markets and

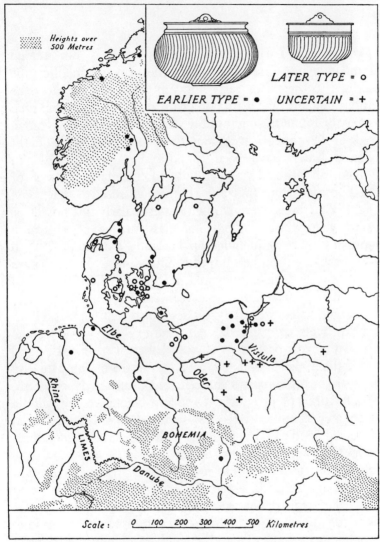

Fig. 12 Distribution of fluted bronze bowls. (*After H. J. Eggers*)

factories of south Russia, linked thus readily with the north. Such is the view of the latest investigator (Eggers), though his

principal predecessor (Ekholm) preferred Italy.[1]   There the
matter may be left until the door is open for further research.

d. GLASS

Under the Early Empire, glassware was not traded
abundantly into Free Germany; some 14 pieces in all can be
ascribed to the 1st or early 2nd century A.D.   Of these the
most abundant type is that of a ribbed or pillared bowl, such
as may be found throughout the vast zone covered by Roman
trade at that time, from Britain to India (fig. 19, 1-2). Eight
pillared bowls have been found, ranging from Oslo to
Poland, all probably or certainly in 'chieftains' graves' of
the Lübsow group (p. 32).   (It may be recalled that some
of the 'Chieftains' were women: a particularly fine bowl, for
example, of white-marbled blue glass was recovered from a
woman's grave at Juellinge on Laaland—see pl. IV, 3, p. 36
—together with other imports, including a bronze *patera*
signed by the well-known maker L. Ansius Diodorus, who
worked at or near Capua between *c.* A.D. 60 and 90.)   The
remaining half-dozen early glasses are conical beakers, either
cut to facets or painted.   An example from one of the
Lübsow graves bears two painted zones of gladiators.

All these glass vessels probably came from Campania by
way of Carnuntum and the central European river-system.
The factories of provincial Germany belong to the Middle
and Later Empire, the glass of which has recently been
reviewed in detail by Eggers, with inevitable reservations
as to the part played by South Russia in 3rd- and 4th-
century distributions.   His maps show a great concentration
in the Danish islands, especially Zealand, a fair scatter along
and behind the Baltic coast as far as the eastern end of the
Gulf of Danzig, a minor concentration in Thuringia,
sporadic occurrences far to the south-east along the Dniester
and in the Ukraine, and a notable extension towards the
north in Sweden and Norway, as far north indeed as the

[1] *Acta Arch.* VI (1935), 71ff.

Silver dish from the Hildesheim hoard, Hanover.　$\frac{1}{2}$
(*See p*. 69)

Silver tray from the Hildesheim hoard, Hanover. ⅔
(*See p. 70*)

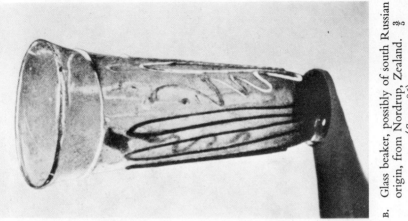

B. Glass beaker, possibly of south Russian origin, from Nordrup, Zealand. ⅗
(See p. 86)

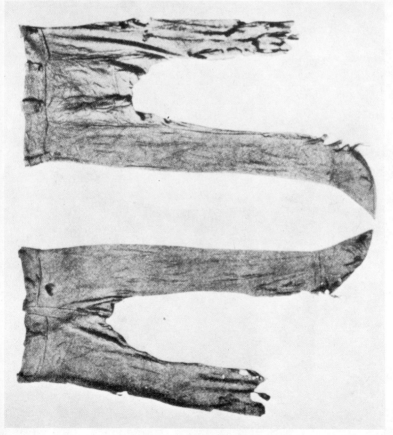

A. Woollen trousers from the moss of Thorsbjerg, Denmark. 1/10
(See p. 58)

A. Painted glass cup of 'Nordrup-Jesendorf' type, from Himlingøje, Denmark. ¾ (*See p. 85*)

B. Cup of green glass with 'claw' decoration, from Vedsted, Zealand. ⅔ (*See p. 86*)

Trondheim fiord.   On the other hand, between the Elbe
and the Rhine, except in Thuringia, only two determinate
glass vessels of the late period have come to light, in spite of
the relative proximity of the Rhenish factories.   The
explanation offered is doubtless in part a right one: that in
the west the dominance of cremation has robbed the archaeologist of any easy source of material.   Against this, however,
must be set the fact that cremation was likewise prevalent in
Norway, which has nevertheless proved singularly productive.   Chance and archaeological skill or enterprise may be
suspected as contributory factors.   Paradoxically, Roman
glass is completely absent from Bohemia, destined long
afterwards to become itself a European centre of glass-
manufacture.   During the brief early period of commercial
prosperity there, glass was rarely traded across the frontiers;
and later, when glass became a major Roman export,
Marcomannic trade had dwindled almost to extinction.

Notable amongst late types which can be ascribed to
western factories are the somewhat rare cylindrical cups,
painted with human figures and those of animals, to which
the name 'Nordrup-Jesendorf' has been given from find-spots
respectively in Zealand and Mecklenburg (pl. XIVA, p. 85).
Nineteen examples of this type have been found, representing
eight localities, all of them accessible by the North Sea
coastal route from the Rhine, with a land-traverse across
the Danish peninsula.   Another type which can be recognized as western by form and fabric is a small bowl with
applied ribs; a type represented mostly in Thuringia with an
outlier east of the Oder.   Other small bowls with cut
geometrical patterns, a type characteristic of Cologne, occur
not only in the Danish islands, Mecklenburg and Thuringia,
but also far away amongst the tributaries of the Danube and
the Theiss and northwards by the gulf of Danzig, a distribution which suggests in part a sea-route and in part a cross-
country route from the upper Rhine to the Danube.   We
have seen that these cut-glass bowls or cups were sometimes
imitated in silver (pl. VIIB, p. 52).   Other types from Free

G

Germany are noted by Eggers as foreign to the Rhenish factories and, with some help from geographical distribution, are ascribed provisionally to the Black Sea markets, though more positive evidence is admittedly required. Relatively tall, slim beakers with applied thread-ornaments, differing from their western counterparts both in form and in the colour and quality of their threads, occur in Zealand (pl. XIIIB, pp. 84-5, in the neighbourhood of the Vistula delta and in the valley of the Dniester, and are thus attributed. They seem to belong mostly to the 3rd century. Two other south-eastern or at least non-western types have a further interest in that they bring Norway and Sweden into the picture, presumably by way of the Dniester, San, Vistula and Denmark. The first consists of small glass cups with claw-like ribs extending from the base halfway up the sides (pl. XIVB, p. 85). This late type has been found on three sites near the mouth of the Vistula, on Bornholm and Zealand, at the north end of Jutland, on two sites in southern Norway and one site in western Sweden. The other type comprises tumblers of thick olive-green glass with cut ornament in which sunk ovals predominate (pl. XVA, p. 100). In date these tumblers come at the end of our period and overlap that of the Folk-wandering, which their distribution in Norway (17 sites) seems to herald or reflect. In this respect they conform closely in time and place with the 'Westland' type of bronze bucket discussed above (p. 80). For the rest the tumblers occur on two Swedish sites, in Jutland and the Danish islands, in Pomerania, at the mouth of the Vistula and in the upper valley of the Oder, thus conforming with the familiar pattern of south-central and south-eastern Europe. Incidentally, a factor in the wide distribution of these tumblers may have been the unusually thick and durable glass of which they are made.

Lastly, a word must be said of the glass drinking-horns with which Rhenish factories supplemented the metal-mounted ox-horns of the German tradition (p. 21). Whether the Rhenish factories exercised a monopoly in this matter is less certain. Glass horns have been found in inhumation-graves in Southern Norway (two), Sweden (one), Jutland (one), Zealand (two), and East Prussia (one), and appear to date mainly from the 4th and 5th centuries, perhaps with emphasis on the later date (pl. XVb, p. 100). The period is one in which, on present knowledge, it is increasingly difficult to allot sources as between east and west, and the distribution is too generalized to help. Once again, the Iron Curtain bars the necessary research.

e. TERRA SIGILLATA

The ease with which the familiar red-glazed pottery known as *terra sigillata* or 'Samian' can be recognized and roughly dated gives it a special value to the archaeologist, and the fact that 262 sites in Free Germany and Scandinavia have produced sherds of it[1] brings it prominently into the present context (fig. 13). Let it be said at once, however, that a large proportion of these sites represents short-range trade to the Frisian coast or up the tributaries of the Rhine. Friesland alone accounts for not less than 42 sites; and the limitations of the trade are emphasized by the circumstance that Denmark, in spite of a century of intensive exploration, has yielded only four examples, whilst on the Swedish island of Gotland, rich in Roman bronze vessels and not lacking in Roman glass, only one bowl of *terra sigillata* has been recorded. This solitary Gotland bowl, incidentally, offers a warning to the student. It comes from an ancient farm-settlement at Känne, on the south-eastern shore of the island, where systematic excavations were carried out in 1926-31 and produced 39 sherds of decorated *sigillata* spread over an area of about 400 sq. m. The fragments cannot be made to join one another, but have been shown to represent a single bowl. It is a cautionary thought that a less careful investigation or a less distinctive vessel might easily have

---

[1] Dagmar Selling, 'Terra Sigillatafynd i det Fria Germanien', in *Kulturhistoriska Studier tillagnade Nils Aberg* (Stockholm, 1938), pp. 101-114; and a fuller list in Eggers (1951), p. 182.

multiplied the distribution-density of *terra sigillata* on Gotland 39 times!

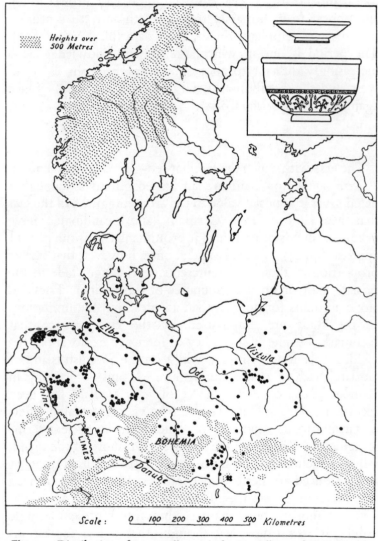

Fig. 13   Distribution of *terra sigillata*.   (*After D. Selling and H. J. Eggers*)

The earliest *sigillata* found in Free Germany is an Arretine vessel (probably early 1st century A.D.) from Holtgaste, Kr.

Leer, in Hanover. The extreme scarcity of Arretine or Italian ware in Free Germany is, however, in contrast with its comparative abundance in Britain (at Colchester and elsewhere) before the Roman conquest. A few specimens of early provincial *sigillata*, made in the south of Gaul between A.D. 25 and 95, have been recorded: notably a bowl of the type known as 'Dragendorff 29' from Vippachedalhausen, Kr. Weimar, in Thuringia, and a dish of form 'Dragendorff 18' stamped OF BASSI CO (i.e. the factory of Bassus and Coelus) from Mehrum near Düsseldorf, and therefore not far from the Roman frontier. Both of these vessels date approximately from the third quarter of the 1st century A.D. Another bowl, made probably at Banassac in South Gaul towards A.D. 100, has been found at Dzwinogrod, Krets Bobrka, in Poland, and is the most easterly example for which a 1st-century date can be claimed. It may have found its way up from Carnuntum on the Danube rather than transversely across north-central Europe.

For the rest, the *sigillata* now in question dates mostly from the 2nd century and was derived either from Lezoux in central Gaul or from one or other of the factories which sprang up in the frontier territories from the end of the 1st century A.D. onwards: at Heiligenberg, Rheinzabern, Blickweiler, Trier and Westerndorf. Thus, one of the four Danish examples (from Valløby in Zealand) is a bowl stamped by Comitialis, who worked at Rheinzabern in the middle and latter part of the 2nd century; a decorated bowl by Cintugnatus, who was at Heiligenberg in the first half of the century, is recorded from Borstel in Saxony; another bowl (form 37) from Dortmund in Westphalia bears the name of the Trier potter Amator, of the second half of the 2nd century; Tarvagus of Westerndorf, mid-2nd century, stamped a vessel from Dambitzen, Kr. Elbing, in West Prussia; sherds from Ciosmy (near Lodz) and Dzwinogrod in Poland bear the names of Elenius and Cintusmus, who worked at Rheinzabern and Westerndorf after the middle of the 2nd century; whilst as long ago as 1776 a bowl of form

37 was recorded from Gispersleben, near Erfurt in Thuringia, bearing the name of Drusus, who worked at Lezoux in the first half of the 2nd century. A few examples of *sigillata* are decorated in barbotine and 'cut-glass' techniques, which may carry them into the 3rd century; but, save for inferior derivatives, the manufacture of this fabric ceased after the first quarter of that century.

If we turn from date and type to distribution, certain points of interest arise. First, the terminal character of the trade with the Frisian coast and its hinterland, extending to the mouth of the Elbe, is sufficiently clear from the abundance of *sigillata* on the *terps* and its absence from the Danish peninsula. It is evident that the Frisians were in this respect absorbers rather than mere carriers. Secondly, the transfusion of wares into the valleys on the eastern flank of the middle Rhine may mostly be dismissed as petty frontier trade, but, on the other hand, some part of this traffic went further afield: up the Lippe, for example, to the Minden-Hameln crossings of the Weser, and along the Main-Fulda and Wetterau routes to the vicinity of the Thuringian Forest, where nearly twenty *sigillata* find-spots recall the considerable concentration of Roman bronze vessels and coinage hereabouts (p. 22). Thuringia indeed appears once more as a rather mysterious island of romanization *in partibus*. Thirdly, reference has been made to some slight evidence—too slight at present for emphasis—that *sigillata* occasionally reached east-central Europe and the Baltic via the amber-route from Carnuntum. Some of the German provincial potteries, notably Westerndorf, traded with the Danube frontier, and *sigillata* sherds found in Czechoslovakia (at Prodbaba, near Prague), in East Prussia near Elbing at the mouth of the Vistula, and, less certainly, the Gotland (Känne) bowl already mentioned have been attributed to Westerndorf and are perhaps more likely to have travelled by way of the Danube and thence northwards than more directly eastwards from the Rhine.

VI · FREE GERMANY: SUMMARY

THE previous sections have shown, if selectively, the remarkable extent to which Roman things penetrated into Free Germany between the 1st and 4th centuries A.D. From that summary much has been omitted; brooches,[1] for example, and pins and beads, in all of which native elements (Gaulish, Danubian, German) are mingled almost inextricably with other elements from the south and west. But detailed studies by categories or localities are not the function of this book and have indeed been supplied in liberal measure for the time being by the lists and maps of Drs. Bolin and Eggers.[2] Here it must suffice to observe the general trends of the evidence which they and others have collected.

That evidence points to three main and in some degree successive sources. The first source was Italy, which in the 1st century A.D. and well into the 2nd century was the manufacturer and primary distributor of most of the Roman goods found on Free German soil. Wares travelled by an adequate road-service to the Danube and thence by the amber-routes to the Baltic or, in the early part of the 1st century, to Bohemia. Here the Marcomanni were for a time active both as ultimate customers and as middlemen in the central and northern European trade, but after the exile of Maroboduus fell quickly out of the running. In the west, the provinces of Gaul and western Germany absorbed Italian goods and passed them on to barbarian buyers by sea and land. Trade was supplemented by diplomatic gifts to native princes, who, incidentally, sometimes reciprocated; as when the Cimbri sought to propitiate Augustus by the gift of a peculiarly sacred vessel (Strabo, 7. 2. 1). War booty must also have contributed to the interchange, but is difficult to isolate. What the Roman traders received in

[1] For these the standard work is still O. Almgren, 'Studien über nordeuropeische Fibeleformen', *Mannus*, nr. 32 (Leipzig, 1923).

[2] See Bibliography, p. 182, and p. 63, footnote 3.

return for their enterprise is almost unknown.   Slaves may
be assumed to have formed a part of the apparatus, although
the human fruits of victory must have constituted a serious
rival source.   Skins may also have been included; Drusus
exacted from the Frisians a tribute of ox-hides for the
equipment of his army (Tacitus, *Ann*. IV, 72), and these same
Frisian ranchers doubtless continued to supply hides or
livestock to the neighbouring provinces.   Marcus Aurelius
received cattle and horses from the Quadi and others (Dio,
LXXI, II).   From Scandinavia, furs and dried fish were
probably traded; furs at least were widely used for clothing
by the Germans, although we have no contemporary
evidence for them in the present context.   Amber from
Jutland and the coasts of East Prussia remained throughout a
primary commercial objective.   But, with all allowance for
these obvious commodities, there is much in the apparatus of
Romano-German commerce that is unknown to us and is
likely to remain so.   Perishable imports to Italy and the
provinces must have formed a major part of it.

Attention has been drawn to the early prominence of the
islands and mainland of Denmark in this traffic, and it has
been suspected that their prominence reflects some measure of
political cohesion, probably with Zealand as its focus.
Whether, or how far, piracy may have contributed to this
accession of wealth in the western Baltic can only be guessed,
but in any case some more regular form of exploitation—
doubtless including control of amber agencies—must be added.

How far Italy remained a source of supply after the earlier
part of the 2nd century is difficult to say.   Our knowledge
of Italian factories in the Middle and Later Empire lacks
precision, and the routes across the Danube may have continued to contribute more than we know.   Certainly,
however, by the end of the 2nd century the second main
source of supply had come into operation: Gaul and the
Rhineland.   Pottery, glass, metalware and coinage now
began to flow thence eastwards and north-eastwards, encouraged alike by prosperity in the west and by central

European wars and migrations which, from the time of Marcus Aurelius, must have slowed down such direct Italian traffic as remained. Here and there an attempt has been made to trace the impact of tribal movement in the map-pattern of Roman commodities, especially coin-hoards, but with very uncertain success. The astonishing bog-hoards of the 3rd and 4th centuries are presumably, however, the product of victories or successful forays on the fringes of the Empire, and again emphasize the dominance of the Danish lands.

The third main source is assumed without close documentation to have been based on Graeco-Scythian South Russia, with extension to Byzantium. Much further research, not at present feasible, is required before the share of the factories and markets of this region can be adequately appraised. Meanwhile, it is rather on negative than on positive evidence that certain categories of glass and metal-work from Free Germany are ascribed to the link established by the Goths in and after the 3rd century between the Baltic and the Black Sea. This link was later supplemented by the impact of the Goths and Huns upon the Empire itself. The phase lies outside the scope of the present book; otherwise it might have been fitting to distinguish Byzantium as a fourth source rather than as a supplement to the third. The great quantities of Imperial gold which now found their way to the southern shore and eastern islands of the Baltic indicate the trends of the time. It may indeed be that, when the contemporary historian Priscus affirms that Attila the Hun ruled 'the islands in the Ocean', those of Bornholm, Öland and Gotland are intended,[1] and that the numerous gold *solidi* found there represent the ultimate diffusion of plunder or tribute from the Byzantine Emperor. For example, in A.D. 435 Attila was able to impose upon the Eastern Empire an annual tribute of 700 lb. of gold, and seven years later the annual levy was increased to 2,100 lb. Established by such means on a vicarious Gold Standard, east-central and Baltic

[1] See E. A. Thompson, *A History of Attila and the Huns* (Oxford, 1948), p. 76.

Europe poised glittering upon the brink of one of the dramatically formative periods of history.

A final comment may be added. What on the broadest and longest view, was the historical significance of this penetration of wares, often of a high grade, far into the interior of barbarian Europe during more than four centuries? Is the study of them merely the laborious collection of *disjecta*, of cultural accidents and curiosities out of context? I think not. They played in fact a very positive part in history. They are milestones on the barbarian road to El Dorado. The subsequent literature of Northern Europe makes abundantly clear the fascination which the Empire exercised upon the minds of those without it. The Empire was the Promised Land, of wealth untold and of perennial allure. Large-scale migration is commonly attributable to economic and social factors based on climatic change, soil-exhaustion, unbalanced population, changing markets, political encroachment. But to these propelling causes which lie behind migration must be added others which lie in front of it, attract it or stimulate it. To barbarian Europe, at least from the middle of the 2nd century onwards, the Empire was in the latter category. Marcomanni, Franks, Alamanni, Burgundians, Vandals, Goths, whatever involuntary rearward forces propelled them, at least knew well where they were going. Traders and raiders and perhaps returning conscripts or mercenaries had already demonstrated the way to fortune. The commodities which we have catalogued marked out the highroads of great folk-movements and advertised along them the delights which lay ahead. Only when at the end of the 4th century the Huns of Asia entered abruptly into the European scene were the main lines of barbarian enterprise bent rudely from the traditional objective. A wedge was now driven deeply into European migration; and thenceforth the tribes of northern Germany and Scandinavia, cut off from the sun, turned their faces with a new determination to the mists of the North Sea. We leave them there and turn our own faces to the far south.

* * *

VII · THE SAHARA

IN recent years the Roman occupation of Algeria and Libya has been the subject of illuminating researches carried out on the ground and from the air by French, Italian and British explorers.[1] These researches require co-ordination and extension, but meanwhile our picture of the organization of the provinces of Numidia, Tripolitania and Cyrenaica has acquired a new actuality, and coherent maps are for the first time available. The present is not the context for a review of this evidence. It will suffice here to indicate certain general features by way of introduction to a more ample notice of discoveries in the deserts beyond the frontier zone.

The mountainous geography of Algeria diversified the settlement of the countryside to a greater extent than did the broader natural partitions of Libya, and at the same time, by canalizing traffic, invited a more definitive system of frontier control. That control was based, perhaps from the time of Hadrian in the twenties and thirties of the 2nd century A.D., on an intermittent artificial barrier of varying design some 500 miles long, linking natural obstacles of mountain and marsh and cutting the approaches into the province from the south-west. A buffer zone was added or organized by the Emperor Septimius Severus, himself of African origin, through the establishment of *coloni* (controlled cultivators) outside a part of the frontier line about A.D. 200; and apart from this specific act there is no doubt that a large share in the

[1] See particularly J. Baradez, *Fossatum Africae* (Paris, 1949); R. G. Goodchild and J. B. Ward Perkins, 'The *Limes Tripolitanus* in the Light of Recent Discoveries', *Journ. Roman Studies*, XXXIX (1949), 81ff.; R. G. Goodchild, 'The *Limes Tripolitanus* : II', *ib.* XL (1950), 30ff.

defence of the frontier was still delegated as late as the beginning of the 5th century to the native farmers, who, as remains of fields and irrigation works show, were settled abundantly in its vicinity.   Details of this native occupation, whether inside or close outside the barrier, are at present inadequately known and in any event do not concern us here.

Further east, however, the situation was at the same time clearer and less closely defined.   Libya falls naturally from north to south into three or four roughly parallel zones: the coastal plain, the broken rocky plateau or *gebel*, and a belt of partial desert best designated as steppe, merging finally into the variable landscape of the Sahara. The first was inevitably the land of the considerable colonial cities, Carthaginian or Greek in origin, later enlarged and supplemented by Imperial commerce. The second and third were the lands of semi-nomadic pastoralists and cultivators, whom it was a task of Rome to anchor both as producers and as a first-line militia.   The fourth was the limitless reservoir of nomadic enemies to all that the settled societies of the Mediterranean stood for.   Had a fixed frontier barrier, a wall or a ditch, been envisaged, it must have stood between the third and fourth of these zones.   But the absence of easy tactical command on the fringe of the desert would have made a huge line of this sort both costly to build and impossibly costly to maintain and defend.   Instead, the frontier zone was patrolled by occasional vexillations or detachments of the Third Augustan Legion (until its disbandment in A.D. 238) and, at least from the beginning of the 3rd century, by bands of local irregulars.   Under the Later Empire, however, defence crystallized primarily into a static complex of fortified farms or *gasrs* in which the farmers of the *gebel* and the steppe increasingly barricaded themselves and so, incidentally and somewhat uncertainly, barricaded the province.   Analogy is presented partially by the Scottish *brochs* or fortified farmsteads of the Romano-British period; more closely, by the pele towers maintained by the yeomen of the Anglo-Scottish border-lands in the Middle Ages.

Through this miscellaneous frontier belt the cities of the coastal fringe received, in varying degrees, the products of the African interior. Ivory, precious stones, gold-dust, ostrich feathers, slaves are mentioned or inferred, and, above all, animals for the amphitheatres of Rome and elsewhere. Some of these commodities were obtainable within the provinces themselves, but some must have come from further afield, transported by the caravans which were the principal asset of the desert nomads. A French historian has indeed remarked that, if Amsterdam be said to have been founded on herring-bones, Lepcis Magna, the great trading city on the Tripolitanian coast, may be said to have been built on the carcases of camels. The proviso should be added that there is no certain evidence for the normal use of the camel in the coastal tracts before the 3rd century A.D.

i. THE FEZZAN

The Roman markets most accessible to this long-range caravan trade were the three which gave Tripolitania (Land of the Three Cities) its name: from west to east, Sabratha, Oea (now the town of Tripoli) and Lepcis Magna itself, all set in a southward re-entrant of the Mediterranean. It was no accident that the hardy column which, under General Leclerc, struggled through from Lake Chad to the sea in 1943 made the coast at Tripoli. Whether the west coast or central Africa were the ultimate goal, the traveller from the Mediterranean would usually make his way southwards to the east-west ridge which forms the spine of the Sahara from the Hoggar on the west to Tibesti on the east, and would tend to travel along it, one way or another, rather than engulf himself in the boundless sand-plateau at its foot. And, appropriately enough, midway between that ridge and the coastal plain, in the Fezzan 430 miles (in a straight line) south of Lepcis Magna, a remarkable assemblage of Roman things was brought to light in 1933-4 by an Italian mission led by Professor Pace in association with Dr. Caputo and

Professor Sergi.[1]   The mission was in the field for little
more than three months, and its results testify alike to
the energy of its directors and the abundance of the
material.

The region in question lies some 50 miles north of
Murzuch, one of the capitals of the Fezzan, and is itself
bounded on the north by the Wadi el-Agial, which runs
east and west by way of Germa, the ancient Garama, known
to Pliny as 'the celebrated capital of the Garamantes' (V, 36).
To the north of the *wadi* (seasonal watercourse, dry for the
greater part of the year) lies the sand-sea, practically devoid
of life; to the south a strip of stony plateau, the *hammada*,
rises to a range of hills, and offers a milieu suitable for
Berber occupation. Here, between Tin Abunda on the
west and El-Abiad on the east—a distance of about 100 miles
—the expedition identified many thousands of ancient
graves distributed in groups along the plain and foot-hills.
Other evidences of settlement in the area, though less
abundant superficially, are not absent. The seasonal rains
of the *hammada* were collected and controlled on a considerable scale by embanked canals (pl. XVIA, p. 101) and
subterranean galleries which presumably represent a skill
imported from within the Roman provinces of the north
(see p. 96). Actual habitations are at present little known,
but a stone-walled 'promontory-fort' commands the *wadi*
half a dozen miles south-west of Germa, and a few simple
square-roomed dwellings are recorded. These various
structures are ascribed tentatively to the time of the Roman
Empire, and a house partially excavated at Germa itself is
more certainly of 3rd-century date, though with Byzantine
repairs.

Of the graves, a majority are cairns, either of roughly
heaped stones or reveted on a rectangular plan with careful
dry-stone walling, sometimes plastered, and with a crudely
domed or pyramidal top. The burial chamber within had

[1] *Monumenti Antichi*, XLI (Rome, 1951), cols. 151-552. Objects brought
back by the expedition are in the Museo Coloniale in Rome.

in some cases been corbel-vaulted with rough rubble-masonry. In front of the tomb was occasionally a bath-like offering-table of stone, with a main oblong cavity and smaller compartments along one of the edges. With these tables might be associated low *stelae*, which sometimes bifurcate into two projections resembling horns. In-humation was the rule, and the skeleton was flexed with varying orientation. But in the present context the important feature of the graves is less their structural form than the fact that not a few of them include pottery, glass and lamps of Roman origin (pls. XVIB, p. 101, and XVIIIA, p. 109). Here a few examples must suffice.

About three miles east of the Germa mausoleum, of which something will be said later, is a cemetery containing a notable tomb of the plastered square or oblong type already mentioned. It had been surmounted by a stepped pyramid, preserved to a maximum height of 4½ ft., with two bicorn *stelae* on the first step of the eastern end. Within was a rubble-faced burial chamber of trapezoidal plan, 8 × 10½ × 10 × 7½ ft., with a depth of 6 ft. The tomb had been broken into previously, the bones scattered and the grave-goods smashed. Nevertheless, the following fragments indicated the former richness of the equipment: two Roman clay lamps of late 3rd- or early 4th-century date; a cylindrical glass bottle with incised square panels, probably of the 3rd century; a green glass cup decorated with simple blue spots alternating with triangular groups of smaller blue spots, a type also of the late 3rd or early 4th century; a cylindrical beaker of similar fabric; parts of a green glass vessel bearing Greek letters; other scraps of glass, a stone roundel or gaming-counter, and two pottery cups with incised recti-linear patterns picked out in yellow, orange and white colours. The pottery cups are non-Roman, but whether of local manufacture is less certain. The Greek lettering suggests without proving an Alexandrian origin for at least one of the glass vessels. The quantity of these in a single grave is remarkable, and indicates a fairly close contact between the Fezzan and the Mediterranean about A.D. 300 or a little later.

A similar but rather larger tomb nearby was of the same general date, and produced further examples of the non-Roman polychrome ware, together with beads and a bone comb, and with lamps, *amphorae*, a glass beaker and other objects from the Mediterranean world. A third tomb of the group was even more amply furnished and was probably that of a lady of rank. It was of plastered, dry-built masonry and retained two steps of a pyramid surmounting a rectangular base about 24½ × 22½ ft. on plan. Immediately east of the tomb was a stone offering table of the kind described above, with the remains of two bicorn *stelae*. Amongst the contents were five red-glazed plates (possibly of the 2nd century A.D.), two *amphorae*, and several plates and cups of cut or moulded glass, one bearing a fragmentary Greek inscription restored on analogy as ΚΑ[ΛѠΣ ΠΙΕ], 'Drink well' or 'Your good health'. More notable are fragments of woollen cloth which possibly represent a purse, and lay on a stone plate in the south-west angle of the tomb. The cloth had been variegated with geometric patterns in yellow, red and blue colours on a purple ground, and was clearly an imported fabric of some value; it may be recalled that dye factories along the African coast are mentioned by Strabo (17. 3. 18) and were doubtless an inheritance from the Carthaginians. The tomb also preserved by chance in its plaster the matrices of two hammers with stone heads bound on to hafts by thongs. Altogether, the equipment was of mixed character and date, but would appear to have been assembled early in the 4th century.

In the immediate vicinity of the Germa mausoleum (see below), extensive cemeteries of somewhat poorer type, with roughly stone-lined pit-graves, produced other imports, including *amphorae*, *terra sigillata* of the 1st century, glass, and clay lamps. Two of the lamps bear the maker's name IUNI ALEXI (Junius Alexius), whose wares are widely distributed in Italy and elsewhere and are predominantly of the

XV

A. Green glass beakers from Ørslev Underskov, Zealand (left), and Killerup, Fyen (right). ⅓ (*See p.* 86)

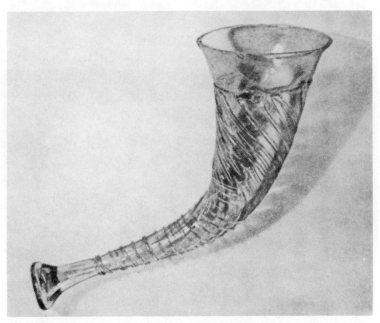

B. Green glass drinking-horn, from Lærkenfeldt, Denmark. ⅓
(*See p.* 86)

XVI

A. Ancient irrigation-canal, Fezzan
(*See p.* 98)

B. Pillared glass bowl from the Fezzan. $\frac{1}{2}$
(*See p.* 99)

2nd century. Another, on the other hand, is of a type common to the 3rd and 4th centuries. Such products occur in sufficient quantity to minimize the survival factor, and it may be affirmed that wares from the Roman world were freely reaching the Germa region from the end of the 1st to the 4th century A.D. or later, with emphasis perhaps on the 3rd century. Similar contacts, if (so far as is known) in lesser quantity, have been detected elsewhere along the line of the *wadi* for many miles east of Germa; and far away at Gat, over 200 miles to the south-west, a cemetery of something like 100 ruined cairns has yielded to cursory examination several glass vessels to which a 3rd-century date may be ascribed: notably, an exceptional polychrome beaker decorated with friezes and panels representing a vine tendril, a wreath, and birds and baskets, probably of East Mediterranean (Alexandrian or Syrian) workmanship.

But at least as remarkable as these fragile imports in the heart of the Fezzan is the famous mausoleum of Germa already mentioned, by far the most southerly monument of Roman type in Africa (pl. XVII, p. 108). It stands alone in the desert, in its trim, classical dignity defiant of the featureless barbarism around it. It was first described by an English traveller in 1826, and, in spite of its remoteness, has often enough been visited since that date. Time and tomb-robbers have dealt drastically with the structure and its former internal arrangements are doubtful, but externally it constituted a tiny shrine with an eastern portico now represented by fragmentary columns and Ionic capitals which, with the gable-ends of the roof, lie scattered on the adjacent desert. The main body of the shrine had at each corner a sketchy angle-pilaster defined by the base and 'composite' capital carved firmly if crudely upon the quoins; it is possible that the shafts of the pilasters were originally indicated in plaster. The base of the three-stepped pedestal on which the building stands is about 12 × 10 ft., and the height to the top of the cornice is 15 ft. The ashlar blocks are excellently squared and fitted, and, save for a provincialism in its

H

carving, the monument might have graced one of the great
coastal cities.

The expedition of 1933 dug out the interior to the natural
soil, and found in the course of their work fragments of
several Roman lamps of the 1st or early 2nd century A.D.,
glass of various colours, Italian red-glazed ware of a type
ascribed to the end of the 1st century, and sherds of less
determinate red and white ware, together with rough sherds
and knives of flint and obsidian of 'neolithic' aspect though
presumably contemporary with the other objects. The
occurrence of obsidian is of interest, since its nearest source
appears to be in the Mediterranean islands, Pantelleria,
Lipari and Santorino. The architectural character of the
monument, its contents where datable, and the general
period of the adjacent burials are all consistent with a date in
the latter part of the 1st century.

The adjacent burials referred to lie less than 1 yard to the
west of the mausoleum and consist of two graves under a
heap of sand and stones, each grave containing a Roman
amphora of 1st-2nd-century type with burnt bones. These
two cremation-burials in a region in which the rite is otherwise that of inhumation are significant, particularly in view
of their proximity to the mausoleum; it cannot be doubted
that they, like the monument itself, represent the intrusion of
visitors from the Roman world, where at this time cremation
was the normal mode.

For the rest, description may here be confined to one other
monument. A short distance to the south of the mausoleum are the ruins of a rectangular dry-stone building
about 70×40 ft. externally with two compartments entered
through the eastern wall. The eastern compartment was
probably a court; the western contained a dry-built stone
tomb, square on plan with rounded corners and formerly
roofed as a truncated pyramid. Externally against the front
of the tomb were six rough *stelae* or orthostats about 2 ft.
high, and again in front of them, in the entrance through the
cross-wall, which was of unbaked brick, was a carefully cut

oblong stone trough or offering-table nearly 5 ft. in length, flanked by two circular stone basins, with a third shallow basin to the east. Burnt bones of sheep and oxen, mixed with sherds of wheel-turned pottery, were encountered in great quantity by the excavators, particularly against the cross-wall, and there were numerous hearths, and at one point a flint knife. In and around the tomb were groups of votive pots, mostly *amphorae* (sometimes incised with Berber letters) but also sherds of red ware, with a stone handmill and a pillared blue glass bowl of a well-known 1st-century type (cf. pl. XVIB, p. 101). These objects extended in depth through an appreciable accumulation of soil and were thought to represent a series of successive deposits and a considerable length of time. Amongst the surface-finds was a fragment of an Italian *sigillata* bowl bearing the head of Diana, and perhaps of late 1st- or 2nd-century date.

This remarkable assemblage, with its distinctive plan and imported wares, would appear to represent a long-lived funerary shrine, of a lower technical grade altogether than the mausoleum, but of a kind derived also from the north and rooted perhaps in Carthaginian rather than in Roman tradition. The extent, however, if any, to which the Fezzan ritual, with its *baetyls* or *stelae* and offering-tables, should be affiliated to Carthaginian practice must remain undecided until far more is known than at present of the ritual of the Punic colonies themselves.

So much for the archaeological evidence as it stands at present from the Fezzan. That it should fit easily or exactly into the episodic history of that region in the time of the Empire is almost too much to hope; nevertheless, the salient historical facts are worth recalling. In 19 B.C. the proconsul Cornelius Balbus celebrated a triumph after a successful punitive expedition against the Garamantes whose homeland it was, and their capital Garama is mentioned by Pliny amongst the cities which he captured. There is a faint echo of a similar campaign, undated, against the Marmaridae further east;

and both enterprises may be seen as moments in the age-long struggle between the settled civilization of the Mediterranean littoral and the nomads or semi-nomads of the mountain and the desert. The antagonism, being of deep-rooted social rather than political origin, was almost incapable of solution, and, in spite of intermittent negotiation, the restless opportunism of the tribesmen long continued to ensure their participation in any trouble that might be afoot. Thus in A.D. 69 a domestic dispute between the coastal cities of Oea (Tripoli) and Lepcis Magna led to the entry of the Garamantes on the part of Oea and the devastation of the countryside up to the walls of Lepcis. The incident was the occasion of the second major Roman expedition into the interior, led this time by the proconsul Valerius Festus, who followed, we are told, a 'short route of only four days' and cannot therefore, at the best, have penetrated far into the tribal area. Writing shortly after the Oea incident, however, Pliny speaks of the Fezzan tribe as 'subjugated', although it would appear that further punitive expeditions were needed to confirm the hasty retaliation of Festus. At any rate, by the end of the 1st or the beginning of the 2nd century opportunity or necessity had evidently swung the Garamantes towards the established rule, for Ptolemy the geographer records two exploratory ventures through their territory (I, 8, 4-5). The date of these ventures is not given, but they must have occurred between the time of Pliny (died A.D. 79) and that of Ptolemy (about A.D. 150). On the first occasion, Septimius Flaccus marched with troops to Garama and proceeded thence southwards for three months into 'the midst of the Aethiopians', a circumstance which suggests vague inquiry rather than a measured campaign. The second venture was led by an otherwise unknown Julius Maternus, under what auspices is not recorded. Maternus set out from Lepcis Magna and came to Garama, whence, with the co-operation of the king of the Garamantes, he led his expedition towards the south for four months against the 'Aethiopians' and reached the unidentified country of

Agisymba, 'where the rhinoceri are wont to assemble'.[1]
Both of these enterprises were doubtless designed, at least in
part, to secure information at source regarding commodities
such as ivory, precious woods and Aethiopian slaves, familiar
to the Roman world through middlemen whose interest it
was to preserve trade secrets and sustain prices. Of these
middle men the Garamantes must have been amongst the
chief, and the archaeological evidence summarized above
suggests that they continued to profit from their position for
two centuries or more after the recorded missions.

A review of that evidence in the light of the historical
episodes suggests a certain measure of agreement between the
two. The Roman imports in the homeland of the Garamantes appear to begin at the end of the 1st century A.D.—
that is, precisely at the time when a sufficiently durable
rapprochement was first established between the Empire and
the Fezzani nomads. The direct interest of the Rome world
in the desert and beyond, expressed historically by the
journeys of Flaccus and Maternus, is expressed archaeologically by the Germa mausoleum, which presumably
commemorates a Roman agent and his companions or
successors established at the Garamantian capital with the
goodwill of the king. It was thus that at an earlier date
Roman pioneers had settled far beyond the northern frontier
at the capital of the Marcomanni in Bohemia with the good-
will of Maroboduus (pp. 8 and 20). But it may be that
another analogy is in fact more apt to the Fezzan episode.
Within a decade or two of the erection of the Germa
monument, Domitian was attempting to quieten the formidable Decebalus, king of the Dacians in central Europe, by
sending him money 'and artisans of every trade, both
peaceful and warlike' (p. 10). Is a similar policy manifest at
Germa, not only in the presence of this surprising monument,
but also and above all in the impressive irrigation systems of
the *hammada* by the Wadi el-Agial? The date of these is

[1] For an interesting discussion of these expeditions in their geographical
context, see F. Rennell Rodd, *People of the Veil* (London, 1926), pp. 322ff.

unknown, but it is difficult to dissociate them from the phase of Roman contact. A primary object of the Roman provinces along the Mediterranean littoral must have been to anchor the predatory nomads, who, on their swift camels, were a proved menace from the deserts of the south. How better to anchor them than by turning them into food-producers, by teaching them to till their own deserts? To the military pacification momentarily effected under the Flavian emperors, a systematic instruction in agricultural engineering was a proper long-term sequel. It is perhaps as likely therefore that the Germa mausoleum represents a Romano-Libyan agricultural technician or adviser who died on a mission to the court of the Garamantes, as that it represents an enterprising commercial agent or a member of what we to-day would call the consular service.

Be that as it may, the evidences of trade are likewise sufficiently apparent in the archaeological record which has been summarized above. The question arises, What was its material basis? What did the Garamantian caravans deliver to the coastal cities in exchange for the wine, the pottery, the cloth, and above all the varied glassware which these remote people prized and buried with their dead? Gold-dust, ostrich eggs and feathers, ivory, precious stones and woods, animals, slaves have been lightly mentioned, but it must be admitted that specific historical evidence is of the slightest. Strabo at the end of the 1st century B.C. tells us that 'the land . . . of the Garamantes . . . is the land whence the Carthaginian Stones [i.e. carbuncles] are brought' (17. 3. 18), and Pliny nearly a century later has a similar story (V, 34). Elephants from the African jungle were familiar, in art if not in life, to every Roman schoolboy.[1] A component of glass, natron or carbonate of soda, is said to occur in the Fezzan and *may* have been exported thence in exchange for the finished products. But it is best to admit that, like the equivalent problem in Free Germany, the economic problem of the

[1] See generally S. Aurigemma, 'L'elefante di Leptis Magna', *Rivista Africa Italiana*, VII (1940), 67ff.

penetration of Roman things into desert Africa is only partially solved.

Of the routes by which the trade was operated, and indeed of the routes followed by the Roman military expeditions into the Fezzan, it can only be said that there are three principal possibilities with a considerable choice of variants. A westerly track led from Sabratha on the coast south-westwards to Ghadames, the ancient Cydamus, near the Tunisian border and thence south-eastwards to the heart of the Fezzan. An easterly track passed from Lepcis Magna through Beni Ulid and Bu Ngem (perhaps the ancient Vanias) to Hun, at the foot of the Gebel es-Soda, which has been identified with the ancient Mons Ater or Niger, and thence southwards to the Fezzan. Between these was a more direct route from Oea (Tripoli) via Mizda and Gheria. This central track, as is shown by milestones along it, was much used in the 3rd century A.D. if not earlier. In the absence, however, of relevant archaeological evidence, attempts to allot the recorded expeditions to individual routes are of no value.

ii. TIN HINAN

So much for the Fezzan. Elsewhere the desert offers yet another problem of a more individual and elusive kind. Nearly 1,000 miles south of Algiers the mountainous backbone of the Sahara ends in the volcanic massif of the Hoggar, to which the cliché 'Mountains of the Moon' might aptly be attached. The emphatic, jagged peaks and craters in their barren setting at the same time repel and fascinate: forming a theatrical background to a strange, lonely tomb which will remain a mystery unresolved.

At the western foot of the massif, not far from the oasis of Abalessa, a rounded hill rises some 125 ft. above the junction of two *wadis*. Its slopes are strewn with rocky debris from the remarkable ruin which occupies its summit. The ruin, pear-shaped on plan with a major axis of about 88 ft., resembles nothing so much as a stone-walled Scottish dun.

(fig. 14). Its dry-built curtain wall varies in thickness from 4½ to 11½ ft., and it contains 11 rooms or courts, roughly oblong save where they conform with the rounded curtain, and standing to a height of about 6 ft. In the eastern wall is a

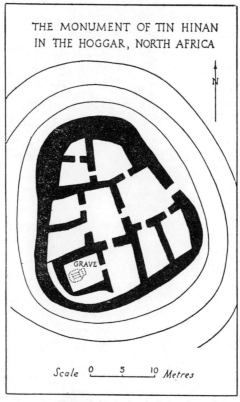

THE MONUMENT OF TIN HINAN
IN THE HOGGAR, NORTH AFRICA

N

GRAVE

Scale 0   5   10 Metres

Fig. 14   Plan of the 'palace' and tomb of Tin
Hinan.   (*After M. Reygasse*)

simple entrance 5 ft. wide. Large iron nails and fragments of charred wood presumably represent the roofing.

The structure was clearly a small fort or fortified residence —palace would be a grandiose term. It has impressed itself upon the minds of the local Tuaregs, and their traditional story has been recorded. Long ago, we are told, there came to the Hoggar from the remote Tafilalet a lady of noble

Mausoleum at Germa, Fezzan. Height 15 feet
(*See p.* 101)

B. Roman lamp from the 'palace' of Tin Hinan, in the Hoggar. Nearly ¼ (*See p.* 110)

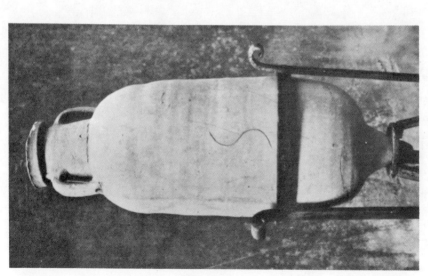

A. *Amphora* from a burial in the Fezzan. About ⅛ (*See p.* 100)

birth named Tin Hinan, accompanied by a faithful woman attendant, Takamat, and a number of slaves. The reason for her journey is not stated, and indeed does not greatly matter. She rode on a superb white camel, and brought with her from the land of the Berbers several loads of dates and millet. But the way to the Hoggar was long, and hunger began to menace the caravan; until one day the resourceful Takamat saw a number of anthills and, dismounting, proceeded to rob the ants of their laboriously stored grain. Thus fortified, they eventually reached the Hoggar, and in some fashion not elaborated Tin Hinan there became the ancestress of the Tuareg nobility. The structure now in question is her monument.[1]

Excavations in 1926 and again in 1933 produced astonishing results. Room no. 1, in the south-western corner of the complex, had been turned into a tomb-chamber or, rather, tomb-antechamber. Its two doorways had been blocked up, and in the floor a number of large flat slabs covered a basement-cell about $7\frac{1}{2} \times 4\frac{1}{2}$ ft. on plan and 5 ft. deep which was the actual grave. In it lay the skeleton of the traditional first queen of the Hoggar, Tin Hinan. The bones, now with the other relics from the site in the Musée du Bardo at Algiers, have been pronounced to be those of a white woman 'strongly recalling the Egyptian type of the Pharaonic monuments, the type of the upper classes, characterized by height, slenderness, wide shoulders, narrow hips and slim legs'. Of that description, all that can be said is that it gallantly meets the demands of the legend.

No less can be said of the other contents of the grave. At the foot of the walls were fragments of matting, in the centre the remains of a bed or couch of carved wood on which lay the skeleton, slightly flexed and facing east, with powdery 'fragments of red leather' which may indicate that the body

[1] For this and an alternative legend, and for the monument itself, see E. F. Gautier and M. Reygasse, 'Le monument de Tin-Hinan', *Annales de l'Académie des Sciences coloniales*, VII (Paris, 1934), and M. Reygasse, *Monuments funéraires préislamiques de l'Afrique du Nord* (Paris, 1950), 88ff.

had been rouged in accordance with a widespread custom. On the right arm were eight bead bracelets of silver, on the left seven of gold; at the left shoulder a small stone cup contained ochre, and by it a little bundle of plants; on the breast lay a gold pendant and beads, white and red, of agate, amazonite, calcedony, carnelian and glass. Behind the head and round the neck and shoulders were about 100 barrel-shaped silver beads, and at the left hip were some 30 other stone beads of various colours. The right foot was surrounded by beads of antimony, and beads of stone and metal were beside the left foot. At the left shoulder, cloth which fell into dust on discovery had perhaps been pinned by two iron pins. Nearby were baskets containing dates and grain, together with two wooden milk-bowls, traces of a coin of Constantine the Great, a gold ring, two small gold balls, fragments of glass with cut geometric pattern of 3rd-4th-century type, and a pendant of polished gypsum representing in stylized form a grotesquely developed female, obviously worn as a fertility-charm. In this mixed assemblage, the Constantinian coin and the glass indicate a 4th-century date and some now undefinable contact with the Mediterranean. The beads are of a rudimentary kind which occurs anywhere from the Ivory Coast to Carthage. The charm is of a widespread class without close specific analogy. The legend of Tin Hinan does not yield to archaeology.

Elsewhere in the little fortress the excavators found a pottery lamp of 3rd-century Roman type (pl. XVIIIB, p. 109), fragments of another, a bracelet of twisted iron and another of bronze, more beads, barbed arrowheads of iron and an iron knife. On some of the wall-stones are fragments of undeciphered Tifinagh inscriptions,[1] in part mutilated by the cutting of the rough masonry and therefore earlier than the building; and at one point a camel and another animal are scratched on an interior surface.

Round about are several small tombs of the so-called

---

[1] The term Tifinagh is used for these characters by the Tuareg, who are themselves unable to read them.

'chouchet' type—that is to say, a shallow pit-grave surrounded by a circular dry-built wall which derives its name
from a supposed resemblance to the *chechia* or Zouave cap.
They contain inhumations, but no grave-goods, and merely
testify to the sanctity of the site.

In the absence of comparable relics within hundreds of
miles of Tin Hinan, it is impossible at present to put her
fortlet and tomb into a wider context. The Fezzan is the
nearest known spot whence Roman goods such as the lamp
and glass could have been obtained, but reason—if such be
expected for an isolated occurrence—is lacking. To postulate
that the structure may have been a rather superior block-
house upon a suppositious trade-route is a mere guess. We
may be content to leave Tin Hinan in geographical suspense
midway between the Roman provinces and Timbuctoo,
and to think of her, perhaps, as a Lady Hester Stanhope of
another age.

VIII · EAST AFRICA

IN the latter half of the 1st century A.D. an anonymous Roman subject from Egypt, possibly from Berenice on the Red Sea coast, sailed the Red Sea and the Indian Ocean in merchant ships and, for the instruction of his kind, set down in unscholastic Greek a factual and remarkable account of the busy trafficking of those parts. His book, the *Periplus of the Erythraean Sea*, is a social and geographical landmark of the first order; I should describe it, indeed, as one of the most fascinating books that have come down to us from antiquity. It will be cited extensively in Chapter IX. Here it is relevant to note the author's knowledge—somewhat vaguer, be it admitted, than usual—of the east coast of Africa, from the mouth of the Red Sea to Zanzibar, and to remark how little his lead has been followed up by archaeological investigation. Turning southward from the Cape of Spices (Cape Guardafui), he takes us in succession to the seaport of Opone (Ras Hafun?), the anchorages of Sarapion and Nikon, the Pyralaae islands, the island of Menouthias (Zanzibar?), and finally the market-port of Rhapta. (The knowledge of Ptolemy in the 2nd century extended over 400 miles further south, probably to Cape Delgado.) The name Rhapta the *Periplus* derives from the *rhapta ploiaria*, boats sewn together with string, anciently a widespread mode of ship-construction which still survives, for example, along the coasts of southern India. The location of the town is uncertain, but is presumably within a reasonable range of Dar-es-Salaam. The interesting information is added that the native ruler of the coast hereabouts had delegated some special measure of authority to the distant trading-town of Muza, near the mouth of the Red Sea, and that Muza sent thither 'many large ships, using Arab captains and agents who are familiar with the natives and intermarry with them and know the region and understand

the language'. This was evidently a survival from the
pre-Augustan era, when ocean trade was still largely in the
hands of middlemen, amongst whom Arabs predominated.

The exports from these east African stations to the Roman
world included, we are told, ivory, rhinoceros horn, tortoiseshell ('in best demand after that from India'), palm-oil,
cinnamon, frankincense and slaves, 'which are brought to
Egypt in increasing numbers'. In return the African
markets received 'lances made at Muza especially for this
trade, hatchets, daggers, awls, and various kinds of glass;
and at some places a little wine and wheat, not for trade but
to secure the good-will of the savages'. The apparatus of
African trade, whether lances or muskets, wine or gin,
altered very little through the ages! Incidentally, the
cinnamon recorded as an African product was probably in
fact supplied by Indian traders. The *Periplus* affirms that
the African seaports were in contact, not only with Egypt,
but also with India, whence ships regularly brought 'wheat,
rice, *ghee* [clarified butter], sesame oil, muslin, girdles and
sugar'. Some of the Indian ships discharged their cargoes
actually in the African ports, but others transhipped them at
sea—a practice due perhaps to the jealous exclusiveness of
Arab middlemen, but more probably to the enterprise of
Arab traders attempting to forestall competition ashore.

Material relics of this far-flung east coast commerce are at
present almost completely lacking. Indeed, only at one
point is there a hint of things to come. In the neighbourhood of Port Durnford, 250 miles north-east of Mombasa,
Captain C. W. Waywood found in 1912 'a walled-in
fortress, enclosing about 5 acres of ground. He caused his
native servants to dig over the top-soil in places and was
rewarded with the discovery of the following copper
coins.'[1] The list comprises one Ptolemaic (3rd-1st century
B.C.), one each of Nero and Trajan, two of Hadrian, one of
Antoninus Pius, one uncertain but of the 1st-2nd century
A.D., and seemingly 79 of the 4th century A.D., amongst which

[1] H. Mattingly in *Numismatic Chronicle*, 5th series, XII (London, 1932), 175.

coins of Constantine I and II and Constans are mentioned. The significance of the discovery is not necessarily vitiated by the addition of six coins of the Mamelukes of Egypt and seven of Egypt under the Turks (17th and 18th centuries). The place may well have been a port of call from Egypt at many different periods, and is certainly worthy of fresh examination.   The Rev. Gervase Mathew, in a letter to the writer, describes it from personal knowledge as 'an almost land-locked harbour on the Indian Ocean, a very suitable waiting-place for the monsoon to India, and on my reckoning the "Nikon" of the *Periplus*'.   There for the moment this alluring problem must be left, pending the emergence of a worthy archaeological successor to the adventurous Greek.

PART III · ASIA

* * *

IX · THE PERIPLUS

IN the previous chapter reference was made to the Greek merchant's handbook known as the *Periplus of the Erythraean Sea*, and an outline of its contents must now be given as a preface to a consideration of Roman enterprise in the Indian sub-continent. Strabo, Pliny, Tacitus, Ptolemy the Geographer, the map known as the Peutinger Table, and the Ravenna Geographer all add materially to the definition of the picture, and picturesque sidelights are thrown from the less factual literature of India itself; but, were all these auxiliary sources lost to us, the *Periplus* would still preserve a clear and comprehensive outline of Rome's remarkable commerce with the East.

By the 'Erythraean' or 'Red' Sea the writer means, not merely the sea now known by that name, but all the seas traversed by this Oriental trade: the Indian Ocean, the Arabian Sea, the Persian Gulf, and even the Bay of Bengal. His knowledge often has the actuality of personal experience and, though now and then it fades apparently into hearsay, its general accuracy is unimpeachable. He begins by describing the commercial harbours of the Red Sea (in the modern usage), and notes Myos Hormos and Berenice, 'both at the boundary of Egypt' as ports 'designated' for some special function[1] which is not specified—perhaps as the authorized channels for certain types of goods. Further south on the same western coast was the important port of Adulis, which also had special legal privileges. From Pliny (*N.H.* VI, 103) and others we know that Myos Hormos and Berenice were both linked by organized caravan-routes with

[1] See J. A. B. Palmer in *The Classical Quarterly* n.s. I (1951), 156ff.

Coptos on the Nile and so with the Egyptian markets. Between Berenice and Adulis, the small harbourless market-town of Ptolemais provided some sort of outlet for Meroe, the decayed capital of Nubia; but it was more important at this time to observe that behind Adulis lay the kingdom of the Axumites, in what is now Ethiopia or Abyssinia, established not long before by immigrants who had been squeezed out of southern Arabia by combined Arab and Parthian pressure. Now, in alliance with Rome, it became an entrepôt of African and Eastern trade, particularly as a focus for African ivory, and received a miscellany of imports which included gold and silver plate for the king and iron and muslin from India.

On the eastern and more barbarous shore of the Red Sea, there was a harbour and fort called Leukē Kōmē (White Town), whence there was a road to the Nabataean city of Petra. The interesting information is added that a Roman centurion was stationed there with an armed force to collect one-fourth of the merchandise imported. Further south and more important commercially was the market-town of Muza, situated not far from the narrow outlet of the Bab el-Mandeb. The region was under Arab rule (see p. 112), but Rome had established trading rights at the town, placating the king with gifts of 'horses and sumpter-mules, vessels of gold and polished silver, finely woven clothing and copper vessels'. The same king controlled the anchorage of Ocelis, actually within the straits, which according to Pliny's informant (*N.H.* VI, 104) was the most convenient port for those arriving from India. This information should perhaps be read in the light of the further statement of the *Periplus* in regard to Eudaemon Arabia (Aden). Eudaemon had 'convenient anchorages and watering-places sweeter and better than those of Ocelis', and, 'when the voyage was not yet made direct from India to Egypt, and when they did not dare to sail from Egypt to the ports across this ocean, all came together at this place. It received the cargoes from both countries, just as Alexandria now receives the things brought both from abroad and from Egypt'. Recently, however, Eudaemon had been destroyed in circumstances that are not now clear, though the removal of the entrepôt to Ocelis points suspiciously to the king of Muza as a party to the fact. Behind the episode emerges the significant circumstance that, whether in the Gulf of Aden or in the actual entry to the Red Sea, hereabouts was a traditional barrier where long-range traffic was withheld from its ultimate Red Sea markets and Arab middlemen took charge. The establishment of Roman privileges at Muza marks an attempt to reduce the costly impact of these middlemen, who presumably still secured their pickings even though (as the *Periplus* states) direct voyages were now undertaken between India and Egypt.

Along the incense-bearing shores of southern Arabia we need not follow our geographer in detail. Thinking back to the rich Roman wares from the undocumented regions of Free Germany, we may again note that the king of Sabratha in the Hadramaut received 'wrought gold and silver plate, also horses, images and thin clothing of fine quality', either as propitiatory gifts or as selected imports. Further, we are told that an unattractive but convenient island, Dioscoride (the modern Socotra), off Cape Gardafui had become a trading-post manned by a few hardy agents—Arabs, Indians and Greeks. Traders from western and southern India brought to this island 'rice and wheat and Indian cloth, and a few female slaves', and took away in exchange 'a great quantity of tortoise-shell'. To the east along the Arabian coast, Moscha (near the modern Taka) was a specially privileged port of call much used in the Indian trade; 'ships returning from Damirica [South India] and Barygaza [Broach in Gujarat], if the season is late, winter there and trade with the king's officers, exchanging their cloth and wheat and sesame oil for frankincense'.

Thereafter our merchant turns northward up the Persian Gulf, at the head of which was a treaty-port called Apologos, later known as Obollah, near Charax Spasini and the mouths of the Euphrates. His information in regard to this region

I

is sketchy and perhaps second-hand, but at such brief times as the Parthian rulers were not at loggerheads with Rome the port must have been an important meeting-place of sea and land traffic. To it and to 'another market-town of Persia called Ommana', apparently on the Arabian shore of the Gulf, large vessels were sent from western India with cargoes of copper, sandalwood, teak, blackwood and ebony, in return for local pearls ('inferior to those of India'), purple dye, local clothing, wine, dates, gold and slaves.

Of all this Arabian trade, based primarily on the export of incense and secondarily on the transmission of goods to and from Egypt and the Orient, scarcely any material evidence of the Imperial period has yet been brought to light along its recorded routes. Little search has indeed been made for such evidence, though regret for this omission is tempered by the general clarity of the written record. No doubt the careful excavation of a site such as that of Adulis would amplify the story in rewarding fashion, and would in particular give a new precision to the Indian contribution. To that contribution the second half of the Greek 'handbook' is devoted (fig. 15).

The *Periplus* first strikes the Indo-Pakistan sub-continent at the shallow, marshy delta of the river Indus, here transcribed as 'Sinthus'. The region was at the time occupied by Scythians under Parthian rule, presumably from the Parthian metropolis of Taxila in the Punjab. At the mouth of the Indus was the market-town of Barbaricum, and inland behind it was the Scythian capital of Minnagara. The site of neither place is known with certainty to-day, though the guess that Hyderabad in Sind, at the head of the Indus delta, may represent alike the ancient Minnagara and the Patala of Alexander the Great is geographically reasonable. The imports and exports through Barbaricum form an interesting list. From the west came 'a great deal of thin clothing, and a little spurious; figured linens, topaz, coral, storax [an incense], frankincense, vessels of glass, silver and gold plate, and a little wine'. On the other hand, there were

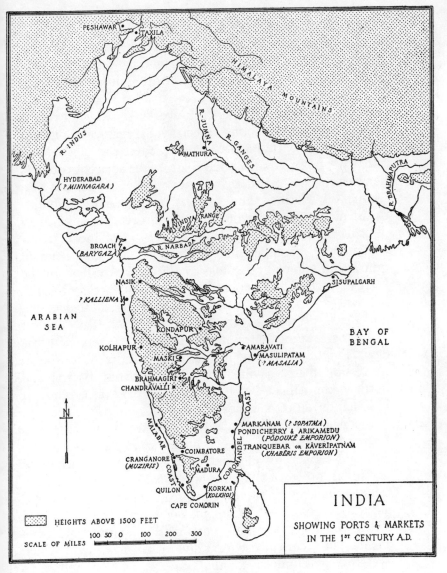

Fig. 15

exported costus (a culinary spice and a perfume), bdellium (an aromatic gum), lycium (a dye and a medicine), nard (a medicinal oil and perfume), turquoise, lapis lazuli, Seric (central or eastern Asiatic) skins, muslin, silk yarn and indigo. Several of these commodities, notably the silk yarn, skins and stones, must have travelled long distances before they were shipped at the Indus delta.   More will be said of this at a later stage.

From the Indus our merchant works his way down the west coast of India, noting especially Barygaza, the modern Broach, on the coast of Gujarat, predecessor of the later 'factory' of Surat on the same coast.   The adjacent country, he observes, was particularly fertile, yielding wheat and rice, sesame oil, clarified butter (*ghee*), cotton and the Indian cloths made therefrom of the coarser sorts.   In spite of its difficult seaward approaches the port was of the first importance in the India trade.   From the wealthy cities of central India it was accessible by the arterial valleys of the Narbada and the Tapti, and routes of no great difficulty supplied it from Rajputana and the north.   Incidentally, the *Periplus* mentions the interesting fact that 'ancient drachmas bearing inscriptions in Greek letters and the devices of those who reigned after Alexander' were still in circulation there, having drifted down from Bactria and north-western India as to-day they still drift (in original or in imitation) into the hands of the Bombay dealers.

Again, the imports and exports are worth noting.   The former included 'wine, Italian preferred, also Laodicean and Arabian; copper, tin and lead; coral and topaz; thin clothing and inferior sorts of all kinds; bright-coloured girdles a cubit wide; storax, sweet clover, glass, realgar [a medicinal gum], antimony, gold and silver coin, on which there is a profit when exchanged for the money of the country; and ointment'.   In accordance with a diplomatic usage with which we are now familiar, 'for the king there are brought very costly vessels of silver, singing boys, beautiful maidens for the harem, fine wines, thin clothing of the finest weaves, and the choicest ointments'. The exports comprised spikenard (a Himalayan herb which produced a valued medicinal ointment), costus, bdellium, ivory, agate and carnelian, lycium, muslin of all kinds, silk cloth, mallow cloth (of coarse, purple-dyed cotton), yarn, long pepper and other things.

South of Barygaza, Calliena (modern Kalyāna, near Bombay) had at one time been a port offering trading facilities, but in the time of the *Periplus* its use was being obstructed by the local ruler. South again, nine other places are mentioned, together with certain islands which harboured pirates. More important were Muziris and Nelcynda, the former of which may probably be identified with Cranganore in the Cochin backwaters; the latter was not far distant, but was situated in another Indian kingdom. These places were in 'Damirika', amended from the Limyrike of the text to conform with the Ravenna Geographer (Dimirica) and the Peutinger Table (Damirika), which shows the region in its Segment XII and marks, incidentally, a 'Templum Augusti' at Muziris. The Roman temple has not been found nor have small-scale excavations at Cranganore revealed any evidences of Roman occupation hereabouts, but the area of potentiality is very large and much further search is required.

The Cochin backwaters are to-day and have long been the home of a remarkable assemblage of races and creeds: communities of Jews, Syrians, Roman Catholics alongside Hindus, each group with its characteristic meeting-places, sometimes of considerable antiquity. The germ of this cosmopolitanism doubtless goes back to the days of Imperial trade, and a Roman temple amongst the palms would accord with the heterogeneous traditions of the scene. The prime attraction to the western trader was the accessibility of these sheltered waterways to the pepper which, then as now, flourished in the hinterland of the moist Malabar coast. Much could be and indeed has been written of pepper and its bearing on the ways of man. To leave the *Periplus* for a moment, Pliny (*N.H.* XII, 14) has an eloquent passage from the Roman standpoint: 'It is quite surprising that the use of pepper has come so much into fashion, seeing that, in other substances which we use, it is sometimes their sweetness and sometimes their appearance that has attracted our notice; whereas, pepper has nothing in it that can plead as a recommendation to either fruit or berry, its only desirable quality being a certain pungency; and yet it is for this that we import it all the way from India! Who was the first to make trial of it as an article of food? And who, I wonder, was the man that was not content to prepare himself by hunger only for the satisfaction of a greedy appetite?' From the Roman world the taste for pepper spread to barbarian Europe; it will suffice to recall that Alaric the Goth demanded 3,000 lb. of it in his treaty with the Romans in A.D. 408. And, to carry the story to a much later date, in 1592 the pepper carried by a Spanish East Indian carrack captured by Frobisher's ships off the Azores was alone worth £102,000. In retrospect it is scarcely surprising that the filling of the Pepper Barns beside the Tiber was a primary function of Roman trade with the Orient.

In addition to pepper, the *Periplus* includes amongst the exports from the Malabar coast 'great quantities of fine pearls, ivory, silk cloth, spikenard from the Ganges, malabathrum [an equivalent of cinnamon] from the places in the interior, transparent stones of all kinds, diamonds and sapphires, and tortoiseshell. This is a fairly comprehensive list. The diamonds, if such they really were, probably came from central India; the pearls coastwise from the neighbourhood of Cape Comorin; the silk by sea from China. The popularity of the market was doubtless due in part to the fact that it could be reached from the Red Sea by a direct trans-oceanic route of which more will be said, with the added advantage that the perils of coastal piracy were thereby reduced to a minimum. The corresponding imports from the west were 'primarily a great quantity of coin; topaz; thin clothing, not much; figured linens, antimony, coral, crude glass, copper, tin, lead; wine, not much, but as much as at Barygaza; realgar and orpiment [a yellow sulphide of arsenic for making yellow paint, from the Persian Gulf]; and wheat enough for the sailors, for this is not dealt in by the merchants there'.

South of Muziris and Nelcynda the *Periplus* is more summary and confused, but the general sequence of place-names probably remains correct. After the Cape of Comari (Cape Comorin) we come to Colchi, famous for its pearl-fisheries, which were worked by condemned criminals; and thence, proceeding from south to north, we reach successively the market-towns of Camara, Podoukē and Sopatma. Of these, Camara is uncertain unless it be a variant of Ptolemy's *Khabēris emporion* at the mouth of the Khabēros or Kāverī (Cauvery) river, where the present Tranquebar represents the former Kāvēripatnam or Kāverīp-pattinam. Podoukē may be equated with Pondicherry or Pudu-chchēre ('Newtown'), near which an Indo-Roman emporium has in fact been discovered (p. 145). With less evidence, Sopatma has been identified with the So-pattinam of Tamil literature, the modern Markanam, on the coast between Pondicherry and Madras.

Ceylon is referred to as 'the island Palaesimundu, called by the ancients Taprobane' but was clearly unknown to the writer, for a reason which will be suggested at a later stage. Meanwhile, we may follow the *Periplus* up the east coast of India, past Masalia, which may be the port of Masulipatam, where 'a great quantity of muslin is made', to the mouth of the Ganges, 'and near it the very last land toward the east, Chrysē' or Golden, presumably the Malay peninsula, known to Ptolemy as the Aurea Chersonesus. On the Ganges was a market-town of the same name, through which were brought malabathrum, spikenard and pearls, and muslins of the finest sorts; and gold-mines and gold coinage (presumably from the Kushāna empire further west) are mentioned.

North of Chrysē lay China, the land called This, 'difficult of access', whence 'raw silk and silk yarn and silk cloth are brought on foot through Bactria to Barygaza, and are also exported to Damirica [South India] by way of the river Ganges'. The *Periplus* ends with a picturesque description of the mongoloid traders who come together 'every year on the borders of the land of This, a tribe of men with short bodies and broad flat faces, and by nature peaceable. . . . They come with their wives and children, carrying great packs and plaited baskets of what looks like green grape-leaves.' One would like to see in this an early reference to tea, but the commodity was in fact probably malabathrum from the Himalaya.

So much for the *Periplus*. Its information is elaborated by other classical writers, but stands first for actuality. Ptolemy, however, compiling his geography about A.D. 150 from a variety of sources including, as he tells us, 'those who have sailed from us to those places and have for a long time frequented them', had nearly a century's further general knowledge behind him and supplements the story. In particular, as we shall see, he knew significantly more about Ceylon than did his predecessor, and his information about the interior of India, however distorted, was not inconsiderable. Along the coast he largely duplicates but also extends the earlier list, and it may be that on one important matter of administration he combines with Strabo, Pliny and above all the *Periplus* to throw a little light.

Round the coast of India and Ceylon, from the Indus to the Ganges, 16 of the coastal towns are singled out by him as *emporia* (e.g. *Muziris emporion*, *Pōdoukē emporion*), which were presumably trading-ports in some special sense. The suggestion is that in each maritime district there was, amongst other places, one which was pre-eminently *the* commercial port, with rights or privileges which it is not Ptolemy's business to define. This recalls the use of the phrase *nomimon emporion* ('lawful market') by the *Periplus* in respect of Adulis, Muza and Apologos, or of *enthesmon emporion* ('privileged market') in respect of Calliena, near Bombay. In these instances there is a clear indication of special legal provision for trading; and some variant of this provision is presumably implied in the word *apodedeigmenos* ('designated'), which the same authority attaches to Myos Hormos on the Red Sea and Moscha on the Arabian coast, though the word may rather indicate the canalization of certain types of traffic through these two places. Two passages in the *Periplus* seem to have a bearing on the matter: at Calliena a new raja had cancelled or at least obstructed rights conferred on traders by a predecessor, to the extent of arresting Greek ships on arrival; and at Leukē Kōmē, an emporium 'for small vessels' on the eastern side of the Red Sea, there was, as we have seen, actually a military post under a centurion to ensure that the Arabs respected trading rights and to collect a duty of 25 per cent. on imports. It is evident, by and large, that the privileges of Western traders were differently safeguarded in the various foreign ports; that in one place (probably exceptional) Roman authority, even a Roman Customs levy, might be guaranteed by a Roman garrison, and that in another the trafficking was subject to the good will of a local ruler, who might be encouraged by diplomatic gifts (pp. 116, 117) to grant and observe concessions, but at long range retained the power to discontinue them. It is likely enough that in the *emporia* were normally posted permanent agencies of the Graeco-Roman traders, organized on lines not unlike those of the Portugese, Dutch, Danish, French or British 'factories' in the India trade of a much later date. Indeed, it is fair to envisage Indo-European commerce of the 1st century A.D. pretty closely in terms of that of the 17th century; that is, it was based on mutual advantage endorsed by Western prestige and sufficiently regulated to ensure continuity.

X · THE MONSOON

BOTH the *Periplus* and Pliny have something of interest to say about the systems of navigation upon which the Imperial commerce with India was based. When he reaches the Indus delta, the author of the *Periplus* records that 'sailors set out thither with the Indian Etesian winds, about the month of July, that is Epiphi: it is more dangerous then,[1] but through these winds the voyage is more direct and sooner completed'. The Etesian winds, as Strabo tells us, brought the summer rains to India, and were in fact the south-western monsoon which begins regularly at the end of June and lasts until September. By keeping it on the quarter, the sailors from the ports near the mouth of the Red Sea were able to steer a tolerably straight course across the approaches to the Persian Gulf, 'quite away from the land', to the Indus and Barygaza. Similarly, those making for Damirica or South India sailed direct a little south of east across the Arabian Sea, throwing the ship's head considerably off the wind and in favourable circumstances making the voyage to Muziris, as Pliny tells us, in forty days. 'Hippalus', adds the *Periplus*, 'was the pilot who, by observing the location of the ports and the condition of the sea, first discovered how to lay his course straight across the ocean.'

Hippalus is one of the great names in the history of navigation. Without his discovery, or at least his popularization, of the monsoon as a dependable aid to deep-sea voyaging, regular trade with India would have been impossible. The long coastwise journey was alike excessively tedious, and fraught with recurrent danger from piracy. The history of the India trade is therefore very incomplete without some agreement as to the date of Hippalus, and agreement has not hitherto been reached in the matter.

[1] The principal danger arose (and arises) from following seas, liable to overtake and swamp small, slow craft.

Our only other historical authority is Pliny, whose account must be summarized and considered (*N.H.* VI, 26). Pliny distinguishes four stages in the development of navigation between the Red Sea and India. At first there was only the long coastal route taken by the fleet of Alexander; small vessels sailed from Aden, along the shores of southern Arabia and Makran, and made the Indus and the west coast of the sub-continent. 'In later times it has been thought that the safest line is to start from Ras Fartak in Arabia with a west wind, the local name for which is the Hippalus, and make for Patale [at the mouth of the Indus], the distance being reckoned as 1,332 miles. The following generation [i.e. the third stage of our series] considered it a shorter and safer route to start from the same cape and steer for the Indian harbour of Sigerus [probably south of Bombay], and for a long time this was the course followed, until a merchant discovered a shorter route [our fourth stage], and the desire for gain brought India nearer; indeed the voyage is made every year, with companies of archers on board, because the seas are very greatly infested by pirates.'

It will be observed that neither the *Periplus* nor Pliny suggests a date for Hippalus. Moreover, whilst the *Periplus* associates Hippalus vaguely with the use of the monsoon in general, Pliny attaches his name only to the second of his four stages—namely, the straight voyage from the Arabian coast to the Indus. Both writers imply that Hippalus was a historical, not a contemporary, figure; Pliny indeed separates him by an 'age' or 'generation' from the third stage, which was in turn a 'long time' before the fourth stage. It is clear that Hippalus lived some very considerable time before the third quarter of the 1st century A.D., to which the composition of the *Periplus* and the *Natural History* may both be assigned.

It is therefore historically unlikely that Pliny's second stage, specifically that of Hippalus, was as late as A.D. 40-1, the date to which E. H. Warmington has attributed it in his excellent book on *The Commerce between the Roman Empire and India.* Other writers, notably W. W. Tarn in *The Greeks in Bactria and India*, have put the Hippalus stage as early as 80 B.C. or even earlier. Without reconsideration of these views, two pieces of evidence which have emerged more recently may be brought to bear upon the problem. The first seems to relate to Pliny's story of the freedman of one Annius Plocamus who in the reign of Claudius (so Pliny implies) farmed the collection of Red Sea taxes. The freedman, while sailing round Arabia, was carried out of his course by northern gales which swept him in a fortnight (*sic*) from the coast of Persia to that of Ceylon. As Warmington remarks: 'Here we have a man who did not know the use of the monsoon winds in order to reach Ceylon.' If from this we take the further, somewhat reckless step of inferring that during a part of the reign of Claudius the use of the monsoon had not yet been adequately advertised, then the late dating of Hippalus might appear to receive some support. Latterly, however, Mr. David Meredith, in studying the ancient inscriptions of the Eastern Desert of Egypt, has drawn attention to an extremely interesting rock inscription, a graffito duplicated in Latin and Greek, in a sheltered spot beside the old road from Coptos to Berenice, at a distance of about 68 miles from Coptos.[1] The Latin version reads:

> LYSA P. ANNI PLOCAMI VENI ANNO XXXV
> III. NON IVL. . . . .

The meaning is clear enough: the graffito is a casual record of one Lysas, a slave of Publius Annius Plocamus, who came that way and presumably sheltered from the midday sun in the 35th year of the Emperor's reign (*Kaisaros* is added in the Greek version). This Emperor can only have been Augustus, and the date is therefore July 5th, A.D. 6. Identity of this Annius Plocamus with Pliny's is not proved and that of the two freedmen is not of course suggested, but the coincidence of the name in so appropriate a geographical setting

[1] *Journ. of Roman Studies*, XLIII (1953), 38.

amounts to near-proof in respect of Plocamus, and it would be wise to consider the date of his errant freedman in Ceylon as likely to have been appreciably earlier than the reign of Claudius.

Be that as it may, of far greater account is the discovery of an Indo-Roman trading-station at Arikamedu, the native name of a waterside tract within a few hundred yards of the Bay of Bengal two miles south of Pondicherry (p. 145), which almost certainly equates etymologically with the 'Podoukē' of the *Periplus* and the 'Pōdoukē emporion' of Ptolemy. The small area excavated here in 1945 yielded 31 sherds of Italic (Arretine) ware, and a score or more of additional fragments have been found before and since that year. Now, Arretine ware of the kinds now in question seems to have been made first about 30 B.C.; more certainly, it went out of manufacture about A.D. 45, and its extensive export to the far side of India may be pivoted on a central date within the bracket, i.e. within the first two decades of the 1st century A.D. But the postulation of a series of trading-posts of this kind—for Pōdoukē was, as we have seen, only one of a series—upon the east coast of India carries with it the postulation of regular trade with the West, and this in turn implies monsoon traffic. The 'Hippalus' may now be assumed therefore to have been in full and undisguised use at the end of the reign of Augustus (died A.D. 14); and incidentally the assumption gives a new actuality to the statement of Strabo, writing under Augustus, that from the Egyptian port of Myos Hormos alone 120 ships left for the East every year.

Whether the 'Hippalus' was known, and if so to whom, before the latter years of Augustus is another matter. It may well have been a trade secret of the Arab middlemen or their Indian agents long before it became familiar to the shipping companies of Rome and Alexandria. The apparent fact that an Augustan tax-collector's freedman had not heard of it does not imply a corresponding ignorance on the part of the professional sea-carriers of Muza or Barygaza. At least as early as the 2nd century B.C. Indians occasionally found their way to Egypt, and a Greek now and then to India; and in the earlier half of the 1st century B.C. pepper was already reaching the Mediterranean in some quantity, probably via Syria.[1]   None of these various circumstances proves or disproves awareness of the 'Hippalus' by Greeks, Indians or Arabs before the reign of Augustus.   Nevertheless it cannot be without significance that the first flood of Western coinage to reach India was Augustan; with it were a few Republican *denarii*, mostly worn, but Ptolemaic issues are unknown there, or practically so, and Strabo (17. 1. 13) observes that prior to his time 'not so many as twenty vessels would dare to traverse the Arabian Gulf far enough to get a peep outside the straits'.   The one certain point, be it insisted, is that the regularization and development of the India trade in the principate of Augustus was to a large extent rendered possible, if not by Hippalus himself, at least by the fact that his discovery and its further implications were now for the first time common knowledge.

[1] W. W. Tarn, *The Greeks in Bactria and India* (Cambridge, 1951), pp. 370-1.

XI · FROM THE INDIAN STANDPOINT

DEVOID though it be of the historical framework of the classical records, Indian literature and epigraphy contain numerous references to these or other contacts with the West. As early as the middle of the 3rd century B.C. the Buddhist emperor Aśoka could write in two of the famous edicts which he had graven on rocks and pillars up and down India that he was, potentially at least, in diplomatic relations with the rulers of the eastern Mediterranean—Antiochos Theos, king of Syria and Western Asia; Ptolemy Philadelphos, king of Egypt; Magas, king of Cyrene; Antigonos Gonatas, king of Macedonia; and perhaps Alexander, king of Epirus. This is a formidable list. Asoka cites it in connection with his proselytizing activities amongst his 'neighbours', but, even in the absence of archaeological evidence, it would not be unfair to suspect that this high-level neighbourliness had a material basis in the form of trade, though material evidence for this is lacking. A century later, Menander, most brilliant of the Greek kings of north-western India, became (then or subsequently) the hero of a didactic historical romance, *The Questions of Milinda*, which refers incidentally to maritime trade with 'Vanga [Bengal], or Takkola, or China, or Sovira, or Surat [on the Gujarat coast], or Alexandria, or the Coromandel Coast, or Further India'.[1] Where or when the *Questions* were first written down is uncertain,[2] but indications point to a date for the oldest surviving version at or a little after the beginning of the Christian era, so that the reference may reflect in part the organized commerce of

[1] T. W. Rhys Davids, *The Questions of Milinda* (Sacred Books of the East Series, Oxford, 1890), II, 269. See also W. W. Tarn, *The Greeks in Bactria and India* (1951), pp. 414ff.

[2] For discussion, see Tarn, pp. 416ff.

Augustus rather than the actual circumstances of Menander's own time. It at least presents India as the focus of a far-flung traffic, which is itself a little suggestive of the later period.

In the story Menander (or Milinda) has a council of 500 'Yonakas'. The number was doubtless exaggerated, but the general circumstance is not unlikely. The word 'Yonaka' is apparently a Hellenistic variant of the more usual term 'Yavana', and is equivalent to 'Ionian', i.e. Greek. The word reappears in a Prakrit inscription at Nasik near Bombay in a Buddhist cave which has commonly been dated to the 1st century B.C., but may be half a century later. Here also and at similar caves at Junnar and Karli in the same region are eight other inscriptions recording dedications by donors who describe themselves as Yavanas. The names of these donors are Indian, and the description of them as 'Greek' presumably implies that they or their forebears had come from cities in the former Indo-Greek kingdom further north; the Yonaka indeed tells us that he was 'Indragnitta, son of Dhammadeva, a Yonaka of Demetrias', a Greek foundation in Sind. In the present context the significance of these circumstances is that they presume a certain preparedness on the part of wealthy Indian merchants of the 1st centuries B.C.-A.D. for further contact with the western world.

Apart from this apparent use of 'Yavana' and 'Yonaka' in a secondary sense, the Yavanas of Indian literature are normally Westerners in the fullest meaning of the term. The Tamil poems of the so-called 'Sangam' age of the earlier centuries A.D. contain repeated references to them.[1] Thus, 'agitating the white foam of the Periyaru, the beautifully built ships of the Yavanas came with gold and returned with pepper, and Muziris resounded with the noise'. In another poem a Pāṇḍya (South Indian) prince is exhorted to drink the cool

[1] See V. Kanakasabhai, *The Tamils Eighteen Hundred Years Ago* (Madras and Bangalore, 1904); P. T. Srinivas Iyengar, *History of the Tamils from the Earliest Times to 600 A.D.* (Madras, 1929); *The Śilappadikāram*, trans. V. R. Ramachandra Dikshitar (Oxford, 1939).

Indian ivory statuette from Pompeii. $\frac{1}{2}$
(See p. 135)

Silver: Indian (3) and *denarii* of Augustus (4)

Gold: *aurei* of Tiberius and Trajan (top row), Claudius (centre), and Nero (bottom row)

Roman and Indian coins from a hoard found at Eyyal, near Trichur, in Cochin State, South India. ¼ (*See p.* 139)

and fragrant wines brought by the Yavanas in their vessels. The epic known as *The Lay of the Anklet* ('Śilappadikāram') describes vividly the quarter of the city of Puhār or Kāvērip-paṭṭinam at the mouth of the Kāverī river—almost certainly Ptolemy's *Khabēris emporion*: 'The sun shone over the open terraces, over the warehouses near the harbour and over the turrets with windows like the eyes of deer. In different places of Puhār the onlooker's attention was caught by the sight of the abodes of Yavanas, whose prosperity never waned. At the harbour were to be seen sailors from many lands, but to all appearances they lived as one commun-ity. . . .' And Tamil rajas employed bodyguards of western mercenaries, 'the valiant-eyed Yavanas whose bodies were strong and of terrible aspect' and who, equipped with 'murderous swords', were 'excellent guardians of the gates of the fort-walls'. In this capacity they are said to have been employed at Madura. Yavana craftsmen were also sought after in southern India, especially for the manufacture of siege-engines, whilst in the north, as a 3rd-century legend has it, St. Thomas was brought to the court of king Gondo-pharnes (*c.* A.D. 19-45) at Taxila for his skill as a builder of 'pillars, temples and courthouses for kings'. In one way and another, the Yavana *in partibus* enjoyed a considerable prestige whether as trader or as settler.

That this various interchange was not unsought by the Indians themselves is clear enough, alike by the presence of Indian sailors and agents along the coasts of Arabia and Africa, as indicated by the *Periplus*, and by the repeated arrival of Indian missions at the court of the Roman emperor. Augustus declares in his monumental record at Ankara that these missions came to him 'frequently'; and, though it is not always easy to distinguish the various occasions from one another, there is more or less specific evidence for at least four of them during his principate. Thus at Antioch an Indian embassy to Augustus was seen by Nicolaus of Damascus and subsequently noted by Strabo (15. 1. 73), who tells us that it came from 'Porus', a king of kings probably in the Punjab, where the name or title was traditional. Owing to the hardships of the long journey, only three of the delegates had survived, but they brought with them a letter written in Greek on parchment together with gifts, including a man born without arms, snakes, a large river-turtle, a partridge 'bigger than a vulture', and a sophist from Bargosa or Barygaza who in fanatical fervour burned himself at Athens and was commemorated there by 'the Indian's tomb' (Plutarch, *Alexander*, LXIX). The Greek letter affirmed that Porus was 'anxious to be a friend to Caesar, and was ready, not only to allow him a passage through his country wherever he wished to go, but also to co-operate with him in anything that was honourable'—a sentiment which suggests the effusive adumbration of a trade agreement. Strabo (15. 1. 4) also mentions an embassy to Augustus from a king 'Pandion', who probably ruled over Pandya, the southernmost kingdom of India. Embassies were apparently received by Augustus in Spain in 26 or 25 B.C. and at Samos in 21 B.C.,[1] and Horace refers to one or other of these missions in his *Carmen Saeculare*. Vaguer references (for example, by the 2nd-century 'Annaeus Florus') tell us of Indian embassies bringing elephants, precious stones and pearls to Augustus; and we are left in no doubt that in his time there was a new rapprochement between East and West unparalleled since the time of Alexander.

Later emperors continued to receive embassies from the sub-continent. To Claudius, as Pliny tells us (*N.H.* VI, 84), came four envoys from the king of Ceylon, 'banished by nature beyond the confines of the world' and previously— as is clear enough from Pliny's account—unfamiliar with the West. The mission is said to have originated from the curiosity aroused there by the castaway freedman of Plocamus referred to above (p. 128). It obviously did not understate the wealth of the island; certainly Roman trade was shortly afterwards extended to it, and Ptolemy in the following century was able for the first time to give an

[1] For these and other embassies, see Warmington, pp. 35ff.

adequate description of it. Again, in A.D. 107 amongst the embassies received by Trajan was one from India (Dio, LXVIII, 15); and we are reminded that in his last years, his thoughts full of Alexander, the old emperor stood on the shores of the Persian Gulf and, seeing a ship sailing away to India, exclaimed: 'Above all things would I have passed over to India, were I still young.' Throughout the 2nd and early 3rd century Indian envoys continued to arrive from time to time. Hadrian received envoys from the 'Bactrian kings', who are probably relevant to a part of our story; and to Antoninus Pius came ambassadors from the 'Indians, Bactrians and Hyrcanians'. Even later, when the Eastern trade was under a cloud, Elagabalus, Aurelian and Constantine the Great are recorded nevertheless to have received missions.[1] The lively interest of India in the Yavanas and their markets needs no further advertisement.

Yet, were it not for the impressive witness of history, the magnitude of this trade would certainly not have been guessed. Material relics of it in the West are few, very few, for the good and obvious reason that most of them were of an impermanent kind. Best of the rare survivors is the well-known ivory statuette of Lakshmi, the Indian goddess of good luck and prosperity, found at Pompeii and therefore brought there prior to A.D. 79 (pl. XIX, p. 132).[2] It is a charming minor work of Indian art of a sort which is commonly, though not compellingly, associated with the Kushāna, capital of Mathurā (Muttra), south of Delhi, and may well have found its way out of India through Barygaza. A case, too, has been stated more than once for the derivation of the squatting posture of the Gaulish god Cernunnos from India, and astonishingly Oriental the posture sometimes is. But alternative explanations are possible and more likely.[3]

[1] See M. P. Charlesworth in *Studies in Roman Economic and Social History*, ed. by P. R. Coleman-Norton (Princeton Univ. Press, 1951), p. 140.

[2] See A. Maiuri, 'Statuetta eburnea di arte indiana a Pompei', in *Le Arti* (Florence), 1938-9, pp. 111-15.

[3] For a documented review, see P. F. Bober, 'Cernunnos: Origin and Transformation of a Celtic Deity', *American Journ. of Archaeology*, LV (1951), 13ff.

The squatting or 'Buddhistic' attitude is indeed a recognized feature of Ligurian sculpture as early as the 3rd or 2nd century B.C. (for example, at Roquepertuse and Entremont in the neighbourhood of Aix-en-Province), and is presumably a native element in this remarkable Graeco-Gallic amalgam.[1]

[1] See F. Benoît in *Gallia* V (Paris, 1947), 81-97; and Benoît, *L'Art primitif méditerranéan de la Vallée du Rhône: la Sculpture* (Paris, 1954).

XII · SOUTH INDIA

THE *Periplus* indicates clearly enough that the traffic with India was basically of two kinds. There were goods which were produced by the sub-continent itself, and there were others which reached the Indian markets from further afield, particularly from central Asia and China. Trade of the former category may usefully be termed 'terminal trade'; that of the latter was 'transit trade'. Although at certain ports, such as Barygaza, the two groups of commodities would converge, they were essentially separate and may be separately considered.

The trade of central and southern India was mainly terminal trade. The spices, muslins, pearls and jewel-stones which constituted the bulk of it came principally from those regions. On the showing of the *Periplus*, there may be added a modicum of transit trade, chiefly in the form of silk which, diverted by Parthian hostility from the more direct continental routes, sometimes found its way deviously from China via the east coast of India to the ports on the Malabar coast and so joined up with the direct monsoon route to the West. We are reminded that, centuries later, on this same cosmopolitan coast a colony of Chinese merchants and craftsmen established themselves and adequately prospered at Quilon. But in Roman times it may be suspected that the China trade normally found its way through more northerly ports in a manner to be discussed presently.

The importance of the South Indian trade with the West in the 1st century A.D. has long been underlined by the impressively abundant Roman coinage which has come to light fortuitously in the peninsula since 1775 (fig. 16). Of 68 finds which (excluding those from Ceylon) are known from the whole sub-continent—India and Pakistan together—no fewer than 57 come from south of the Vindhyas; and, with the exception of a stray *denarius* of Tiberius at Taxila in the

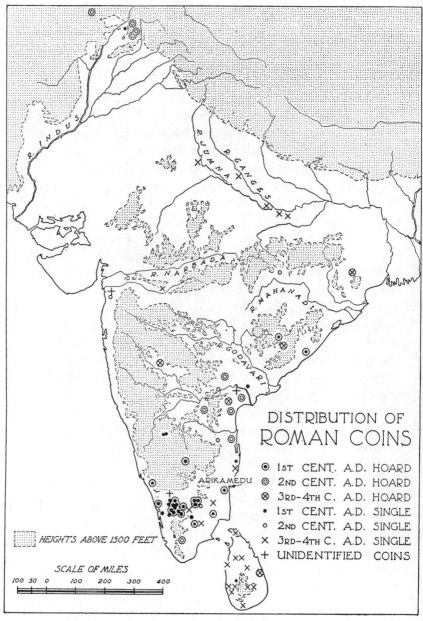

DISTRIBUTION OF
ROMAN COINS

⊙ 1ST CENT. A.D. HOARD
⊚ 2ND CENT. A.D. HOARD
⊗ 3RD-4TH C. A.D. HOARD
• 1ST CENT. A.D. SINGLE
○ 2ND CENT. A.D. SINGLE
✕ 3RD-4TH C. A.D. SINGLE
+ UNIDENTIFIED COINS

ARIKAMEDU

⌗ HEIGHTS ABOVE 1500 FEET

SCALE OF MILES
100 50 0   100   200   300   400

R. INDUS
R. JUMNA
R. GANGES
R. NARBADA
R. MAHANADI
R. GODAVARI

Fig. 16

Punjab, *all* 1st-century Roman coins not associated with later issues have been found in the south. More precisely 29 finds, distributed through Madras province and the states of Hyderabad, Mysore, Cochin, Pudukottai and Travancore, comprise *aurei* or *denarii* ranging from Augustus to Trajan (pl. XX, p. 133). This mass of coinage demands analysis.

The first noteworthy point is that, of the 29 1st-century finds, at least 20 are known to have constituted hoards, ranging individually from four or five coins to 'some hundreds, if not thousands'. In the circumstances it is reasonable to suspect that some of the ill-recorded strays likewise represent hoards.

Secondly, these 1st-century coins are invariably of gold or silver. There is no authenticated discovery of a Roman 'brass' coin of the 1st or 2nd century in India.

Thirdly, coins of Augustus and Tiberius predominate. After Nero they dwindle markedly.

Fourthly, the gold coins are liable to be either pierced for suspension or mutilated by a cut across the obverse. Only one of the very numerous Roman silver coins is known to have been similarly mutilated.

Fifthly, there is a notable grouping of early coin-finds across southern India from the western to the eastern coasts.

Of these five points, the first is readily explained in relation to the second. The significance of hoards in general has often been discussed, and they are commonly regarded as savings lost, or rather not recovered, during a period of disturbance. But it would be easy to overstress this aspect of the matter, and, whatever the accidents of their final deposition, it may be suggested that the preponderance of early Roman hoards in South India first and foremost represents an essentially economic factor. The great quantity of gold and silver coins imported by 1st-century Roman trade into India is noted or implied by more than one classical writer. The *Periplus* mentions it in relation to Barygaza and as first amongst the imports carried by Western merchants to the Malabar ports; Pliny (VI, 101) remarks that 'in no year does India absorb less than fifty million sesterces', which presumably represented actual cash rather than the estimated value of wares; Tiberius may be thought to have had this extravagant efflux specially in mind when he complained to the Roman senate of the reckless exportation of money 'to foreign nations and even to the enemies of Rome' in exchange for gew-gaws (Tacitus, *Ann.* II, 53). But how was all this currency fitted into the alien economies of recipients far beyond the boundaries of the Roman Empire?

The clear answer is that, for the most part, it was employed not as currency but as bullion. In the whole of peninsular India there was no native currency of gold or silver to which the Roman coinage could be approximated. Pausanias (III, 12, 24) in the 2nd century observed that the Indians exchanged their wares with those of the Greeks without understanding the use of money. The potin or lead coinage struck by the Andhra empire of central India in the first two centuries A.D. is a partial exception to this rule; and half a dozen scattered denarii of Augustus and Tiberius found over a period of years in a restricted area of an Andhra town at Chandravalli, near Chitaldrug in northern Mysore, if they do not represent a hoard broken anciently, may here have circulated in some ratio to the native base-metal issues. Outside the Andhra zone, however, this possibility does not arise. For the most part, the imported coins can only have been used as bullion, to be weighed out in exchange for goods as silver ornaments or scraps may be weighed out in an Indian bazaar to-day. Their normal occurrence in 'hoards' is a natural corollary. Indeed, the term 'hoard' is in this context largely a misnomer; the so-called hoard being doubtless a unit of stamped silver or gold to a total weight agreed for some specific purchase, or at least the bulk reserve from which such units could be detached. Monetary circulation in the ordinary sense was not in question. The fact that the precious metal was already subdivided into known and stamped sub-units (coins) would

Site of Indo-Roman trading-station at Arikamedu,
near Pondicherry, South India
(*See p.* 145)

A. Arikamedu: brick foundations projecting from river-bank. (*See p.* 145)

B. Arikamedu: excavations in progress, 1945. (*See p.* 145)

Arikamedu: fragments of Roman *amphorae*.   ⅔
(*See* p. 146)

Arikamedu: 1-6, fragments of Arretine dishes (1 stamped VIBIE);
7, fragment of Roman lamp. $\frac{3}{4}$
(*See p.* 149)

nevertheless facilitate the trader's accounting and at the same time carry prestige with the customer. Pliny (VI, 85) tells a relevant story of the admiration expressed by the king of Ceylon for Roman honesty, on the ground that among the money found on a Roman castaway (Plocamus's famous freedman) the *denarii* were all equal in weight, although the various figures on them showed that they had been coined by several emperors.

This respect for Roman integrity was evidently shaken in India, as in Free Germany (p. 66), by Nero's debasement of his silver coinage in A.D. 63. The third of our points above needs no additional explanation. Just as in Free Germany the older pre-Neronic issues in pure silver were sought in preference to the alloyed issues subsequent to the year 63, so in India silver issues later than Nero hardly occur, whilst several hoards end with his reign or that of his predecessor. And to this shaken confidence on the Indian side in the bullion value of the newer *denarii* may certainly be added export restrictions at source, arising from the expressed anxiety of the Roman treasury at the enormous outflow. That the India trade continued or even increased after the time of Nero is clear from Ptolemy and from the recent archaeological evidence of Arikamedu, which will be considered below. But it continued mainly in manufactured goods and raw materials with only a modest reinforcement from Roman gold and (much later) base metal.

This brings us to our fourth point, the mutilation of the gold coinage (two examples in pl. XX, p. 133). The facts are as follows. Apart from occasional coins pierced for use as ornaments or charms, in at least six of the hoards the gold coins have, wholly or mostly, been defaced by an incision across the imperial head; and, since no other feature of the design, even when representation of the human figure is involved, has been singled out for this treatment, the purpose of the defacement was definitely not iconoclasm, but the cancellation of the piece as a coin-issue. The defaced coins cover a wide range of time, including issues of Claudius,

Nero, Vespasian, Hadrian and, apparently in one case, Constantine I.

For this mutilation there is no need to question the explanation long ago put forward by Sir George Hill that 'the incisions were made in India, in order to put the coins out of circulation'.[1] But an interesting fact may be added. Except in one *stūpa*-deposit, which as a votive offering may be regarded as a law unto itself, none of this Roman gold, whether mutilated or not, is found within the probable limits of the late 1st- and 2nd-century Kūshāna empire, which included the whole of north-western India and the west-coast trading-ports of the Indus delta, Gujarat and Bombay. *Within* that empire was at this time struck the only native gold coinage of the period in India, and it was struck significantly to the Roman standard. In other words, it was in unconcealed competition with the Roman coinage, and the suggestion has even been made that it consisted, at any rate in part, of re-struck Roman *aurei*. The implication is that all Roman gold which could be recovered was absorbed by the Kushāna empire and thus regulated or reminted; and the all-powerful Kushāns saw to it that such Roman gold as was admitted to their border states was removed by mutilation from possible rivalry as currency, and relegated to use as bullion or ornament. The fact that most of this Roman gold is of 1st-century date, whereas the Kushāna empire reached its prime in the 2nd century is readily explained by Roman export restrictions from the latter part of the 1st century onwards and the consequence that little more than gold surviving in trade from the previous period was now in use.

The fact that a minority of the Roman gold was not mutilated implies, on this showing, merely the unequal reach of Kushāna interference or a measure of administrative laxity that requires no explanation in the East. In regard to imported silver, the question did not arise. As already remarked, no silver coinage comparable with the imported

[1] *Num Chron.*, 3rd Series, XVIII (1898), 320; modified, *ib.* XIX (1899), 82.

denarii existed in India in the 1st or 2nd century A.D.;
even the Kushāns issued none, with a single exception of
Kadphises II in the British Museum and four coins, also
unique, probably of his predecessor Kujūla Kadphises from
Taxila.[1] Thus, unless very doubtfully in the Andhra
kingdom, there was little risk of the intrusion of the *denarius*
as currency since the country, including the Kushāṇa
empire, was as a whole economically unprepared for it.

We may now turn to our fifth point, geographical distribution. Be it repeated that a large proportion of the Roman
coins from India has been found in the peninsula, to the south
of the Vindhyas and even to the south of the main Deccan
plateau. Within this vast area, the district of Coimbatore
and its borders, some 250 miles south-west of Madras, have
produced more than the whole of the rest of the sub-continent put together. From the Coimbatore district alone
there are at least 11 1st-century hoards, running in the
aggregate to many hundreds of gold and silver coins. As
in all such cases, the first step is to refer to the map.

The district of Coimbatore is approached up two major
river-valleys, that of the Cauvery from the east coast and
that of the Ponnani from the west. It lies at the point where
the Eastern Ghats, swinging westwards, merge into the
Western Ghats and conspire with them to leave a transverse
gap, about 20 miles wide and only 1,000 ft. high, between
east and west. To-day through this, the Ponnani or
Pālghāt or Coimbatore gap, the railway from Madras and
the Carnatic plain penetrates to Calicut and Cochin; and the
traditional use of this route is indicated by the legend which
lands St. Thomas on the Malabar coast near Cranganore and
takes him thence overland to the Madras coast.[2] Along this
same route crowd the coins now in question (fig. 17).
Along it at first, we cannot doubt, came the ancient traffic
from Muziris (Cranganore) and Nelcynda to *Pōdoukē
emporion* and *Khabēris emporion* (Arikamedu and Tranquebar)
on the opposite coasts, evading the dangerous voyage round

[1] J. Marshall, *Taxila* (Cambridge, 1951), I, 68. [2] Warmington, p. 83.

Cape Comorin.   The avoidance of circumpeninsular navigation was a habit of ancient travelling.   The little Cornish
peninsula and the Jutland peninsula were thus short-circuited
at one time or another.   So too was peninsular India.
Strabo in the time of Augustus wrote (15. 1. 4) that in his
day only stray individuals had sailed round India to the
Ganges and that they were 'of no use as regards the history
of the places they had seen'.   Pliny, as already related, had no

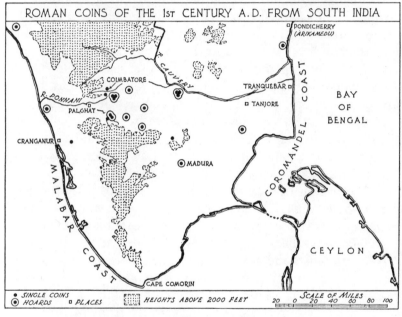

Fig. 17

recent knowledge of Ceylon until the embassy from the
king of the island came to Rome with scrappy information
in the time of Claudius.   The *Periplus* becomes noticeably
vague when, southbound, it leaves Nelcynda on the Malabar
coast.   Indeed Ptolemy, in the middle of the 2nd century
A.D., is our first circumstantial authority for those parts, and
it has been observed that, in writing of Ceylon, he appears to
have been making a display of information that was largely
new to his reader.   It is a fair inference that the Roman

agencies established in the east coast ports under Augustus and Tiberius were, so far as the Westerners were concerned, the termini of trans-peninsular routes, and that only towards the end of the 1st century were the western and eastern ports linked also by regular circumpeninsular traffic. Consistently with this, no coins earlier than Nero and Vespasian are recorded from Ceylon.

If there are, then, clear geographical reasons for the short-circuiting of wealth and traffic through Coimbatore, it is fair to ask why did so appreciable a proportion of it come to rest there? The question cannot at present be answered. According to an unconfirmed but plausible Tamil tradition, the three ancient kingdoms of South India—Chola, Chera and Pandya—met in the Coimbatore district, and such a convergence of frontiers, providing alternative escapes, is at all times a favourite focus of brigandage. The hiding and loss of some part of this bullion would fit easily enough into that picture. Other hoards may represent the forgotten treasury of local prospectors and miners concerned with the famous beryl mines of the district, or of the owners of the pepper estates which doubtless spread, as to-day, on and below the 3,000-ft. contour in the fringes of the district. There is reason to suppose that search would reveal ample evidence of occupation hereabouts, and excavation is now the necessary preliminary to further knowledge. Only at the eastern end of the zone, on the Coromandel Coast, has serious digging so far been attempted, and here the results have been immediate and dramatic.

Two miles south of Pondicherry, the capital of French India, a former outlet of the Gingee river forms a lagoon locked to-day by a sand-bar from the Bay of Bengal, from which it is further sheltered by dunes and coconut palms. A part of the eastern bank of the lagoon stands some 20 ft. above the water and from the scarp project the jagged ends of successive brick buildings to which the mound owes its being (pls. XXI-XXIV, pp. 140-1). To the villagers the site is known as Arikamedu; French archaeologists have preferred to name it from a neighbouring village, Viram-patnam. The fragments of walling were noted as long ago as the 18th century, but it was in 1937 that the site first attracted archaeological attention.

In that year village children brought to a local French antiquary a number of relics which they had picked up on the surface, amongst them a gem (now lost) which is reported to have borne an intaglio portrait of Augustus. Sub-sequently French and Indian investigators carried out some useful if summary digging on the site, and amongst the resultant finds the present writer in 1944 detected sherds of Italian red-glazed 'Arretine' ware and of *amphorae* from the Mediterranean, together with a fragment of a Roman lamp and a second Graeco-Roman gem, an untrimmed crystal intaglio representing a cupid and a bird. The Arretine ware was of the early 1st century A.D. In 1945 a systematic excavation was carried out for three months by the Archaeological Survey of India under the writer's direction, and the work was resumed for the French Govern-ment by Mr. J. M. Casal in 1947-8.[1] The accumulated material of Western origin supplements with important detail the general historical and numismatic evidence given above, whilst, from the Indian standpoint, it has for the first time provided a firm and widely applicable datum for the associated native culture. The excavations have thus com-bined in a happy manner the interests alike of Western and of Indian archaeology.

Much of the town has been removed by the river, and its former landward extent is unknown, but the excavations of man and nature have identified a nucleus over 400 yards from north to south along the bank. Under the southern part of this area have been found the traces of a village associated with smooth black-and-brown pottery of the

---

[1] For the 1945 and earlier work, see *Ancient India*, No. 2 (Delhi, 1946), pp. 17ff.; for the 1947-8 work, see J. M. Casal, *Fouilles de Virampatnam-Arikamedu* (Paris, Imprimerie Nationale, 1949); also *Aspects of Archaeology (Essays to O. G. S. Crawford)* (London, 1951), pp. 354ff.; and *Germania* 1952, p. 389.

distinctive kind used by the builders of megalithic tombs in South India between *c.* 200 B.C. and A.D. 50. This village, like its modern equivalents in the neighbourhood, doubtless consisted of simple fisher-folk who caught the gullible fish of the region from the shore or from small outriggers, gathered the fruits and juices of the palms, cultivated rice-patches, and lived in a leisurely and unenterprising fashion just above subsistence level. To it suddenly, from unthought-of lands 5,000 miles away, came strange wines, table-wares far beyond the local skill, lamps of a strange sort, glass, cut gems. Traders arrived across-country from the west coast to meet the large Indian east coast ships of which the *Periplus* tells us, laden with gemstones from Ceylon, pearls from Kolchoi (Colchi), or spices and silks from the Ganges. A small foreign quarter like that of Puhar (p. 133) came into being, and finally the village was replaced by a brick-built town, spreading north-wards to the sea. There is no reasonable doubt that this *new town* was the *Podoukē* of the *Periplus*, the *Pōdoukē emporion* of Ptolemy, the Pudu-chcheri or 'New Town' of the Tamils, garbled by Europeans as Puddicherry and Pondi-cherry. Shifting sands have moved the town a mile or two, but the name has come down, little changed, through nineteen centuries.

Of the buildings of this New Town something is now known, although brick-robbers have upturned much of the site. At the northern or seaward end, beside the river and at water-level, was a large, simple brick structure upwards of 150 ft. long, pretty obviously a warehouse. Further south were courtyards walled with brick and timber, containing stoutly constructed brick tanks and cisterns, drains, wells and soak-pits, the last made in a characteristically Indian fashion of superimposed terracotta rings. South again, a formidable brick revetment, sloped or battered and surviving to a height of 6 ft., was traced by Mr. Casal for a distance of 80 yards eastwards from its broken end on the river bank and was interpreted as the side of a tank or reservoir, but may rather have been a defensive revetment. And still further south scraps of walling have come to light in the much-disturbed ground. The overall impression is that of storage-accommodation towards the mouth of the former estuary, backed by industrial quarters where, it may be supposed, the 'Agaritic' muslins which the *Periplus* mentions as an export of the region were made and dyed, and where beads and other objects of semi-precious stones, which litter the area, were assembled or worked. The administrative centre, temples and dwellings of the town have not yet been identified.

Most of the brick buildings explored were constructed after the red-glazed Arretine ware had ceased to arrive from Italy, where its manufacture, in the forms and fabric now in question, came to an end about A.D. 45. On the other hand the importation of wine-*amphorae* seems to have preceded that of the Arretine and certainly continued after the Arretine had ceased. The main development of the port may in fact be ascribed approximately to the middle of the 1st century A.D., although its international usage must have begun nearly half a century earlier, if the depth of the deposit (9 ft.) containing *amphora* sherds under the warehouse be taken as an index.[1] Moreover, some of the Arretine ware dates probably from the first quarter of the 1st century A.D. For the subsequent duration of the town we have at present insufficient evidence. In the industrial area where the tanks or dye-vats are situated there were two or more phases of reconstruction, but there was a general continuity in the main units of the plan, and sherds of Mediterranean amphora occurred in all strata. In other words, the function and contacts of the site remained unchanged. To interpret these factors in terms of time is guesswork; a minimum of a century might appear to have been required by the renewals, but there seems to be no compelling reason to allow more than two centuries, and a terminal date soon after A.D. 200 is suggested.

The quantity of Western pottery in the relatively small

[1] This deposit was largely alluvial mud and probably accumulated fairly rapidly.

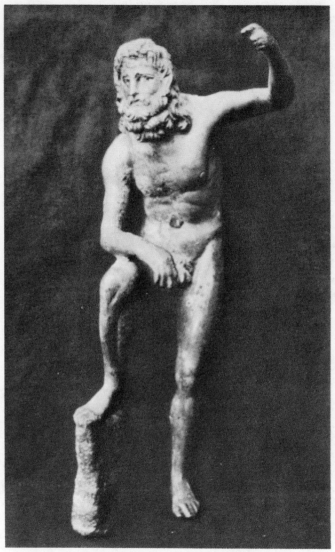

XXV

Bronze statuette of Poseidon from Kolhapur, Western India. $\frac{1}{4}$
(*See p. 151*)

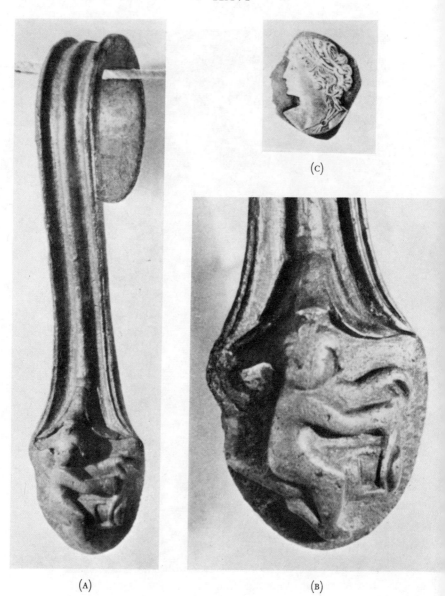

XXVI

(C)

(A)   (B)

A and B.   Handle of bronze jug from Akota, Baroda, Western India.
   C.   Cameo from Karvan, Baroda, Western India.   Nearly ¼
(*See pp.* 151-2)

areas uncovered is impressive (pls. XXIII and XXIV, pp. 140-1). At least fifty sherds of Arretine, including four potters' stamps (VIBIE, ITTA, CAMVRI, C.VIBI OF) are recorded, and others have been found, mostly in the northern (warehouse) sector where, it may be supposed, the shippers and merchants were congregated. Of *amphora* sherds something like 150 are known to have been unearthed over a wider area; and incidentally an internal incrustation on some of the sherds has been shown by analysis to contain resin, a traditional component of certain Greek wines though here (as elsewhere) perhaps applied deliberately by the potters to render the

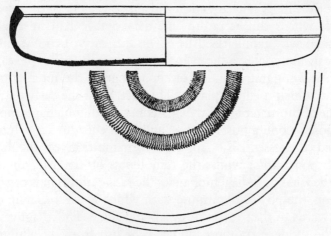

Fig. 18   Rouletted dish from Arikamedu.   ¼

vessels impermeable.   Other wares which may have been imported from the West include above all an extensive group of flat-bottomed dishes of a hard, metallic pottery, whitish in section but with a polished slip blackened internally by inverted firing and with concentric rings of rouletting on the upper surface of the base (fig. 18).   Local imitations of this ware are distinguished by softer fabric and coarser rouletting.   This 'rouletted dish' is widely distributed in southern and central India and has become what geologists would call a 'type fossil' in the dating of associated Indian cultures.   It will be considered again at a later stage.

L

Roman glass, including a 'pillared' bowl of 1st-century type (fig. 19, 2), reached the site in small quantities, and fragments of at least two characteristic Roman lamps of early date have been noted. On the other hand, coins of the period, whether Roman or Indian, are completely absent. This is in accordance with the postulate, already discussed, that the imported currency was not as a rule circulated in India in the normal processes of monetary exchange, the country being economically unprepared for it.

The discovery of Arikamedu is in more than one respect a landmark in the study of Indo-Roman relations. For the first time it gives a habitation and a name to one of the *emporia* with which the literature and the coinage had in a more general way familiarized us. The quantity of the Mediterranean material produced by comparatively trifling excavation is a suggestive index of the extent of the international trade which used the place. This fact, with the early date of some of the material and the suddenness with which it is superimposed upon a purely native and local culture, has substantiated the essentially Augustan organization of regulated monsoon traffic; whilst the remoteness of the site, on the further side of India, emphasizes the range of this new organization, the powerful purpose with which it was reaching out eastwards to the sources of pearls and silk. The imagination of the modern enquirer kindles as he lifts from the alluvium of the Bay of Bengal sherds bearing the names of craftsmen whose kilns lay on the outskirts of Arezzo. From the woods of Hertfordshire to the palm-groves of the Coromandel, these red-glazed cups and dishes symbolize the routine adventures of tradesmen whose story may be set only a little below that of king Alexander himself.

Other sites in central and southern India have produced occasional evidence of direct or indirect contact with Roman things, but cannot at present be classed with Arikamedu. Reference has been made to the rouletted dishes which were first identified and dated there, and to their distinctively Mediterranean character even when they may in fact be local copies. This type, wholly foreign to Indian ceramic tradition, nevertheless 'caught on' in India and has become an invaluable index of date on many sites where other time-evidence is lacking or inadequate. Far from the coast in northern Mysore, on the great central plateau, it has been found with, and has helped to date, an Andhra town of the 1st and 2nd century A.D. at Brahmagiri in the Chitaldrug district; and 45 miles away in the same district it has appeared at Chandravalli where, appropriately, denarii of Augustus and Tiberius have likewise been found. The Andhra towns of Maski and Kondapur, also on the Deccan plateau, have produced similar sherds; whilst nearer the east coast at yet another Andhra city, Amaravati, more rouletted pottery has been gathered on the surface, and the same site is said long ago to have yielded Roman coins not otherwise specified. Here, beside the famous *stūpa* which provided the sculptures long exhibited on the main staircase of the British Museum, is a town site which from more than one standpoint would amply repay excavation. And away to the north-east, some 700 miles from Arikamedu, near the sacred temple-city of Bhubaneswar, the excavators of an ancient walled town known as Sisupalgarh have found sherds of the same ware. These widespread occurrences represent altogether but a brief period of fieldwork, and there is no doubt that our new 'type fossil' of the 1st century A.D. will acquire an increasing importance as time goes by.

Apart from the rouletted ware, red-glazed pottery of non-Indian, Mediterranean type has recently been found at Nasik, near Bombay. More manifestly Western in origin are a bronze statuette of Neptune or Poseidon and a Roman bronze jug of the middle of the 1st century A.D. from another site not far from the west coast (pls. XXV and XXVIIA, pp. 148 and 156). They were found together in a brick building of Andhra date in an ancient town-mound at Kolhapur in the southern part of Bombay province, and are striking evidences of the trade which, as our historical authorities indicate, used a number of harbours on the

Konkan coast, south of Bombay. When last seen by the writer in 1948 the jug and statuette were housed in a little museum at Kolhapur. The statuette is of better quality than the average commercial product and, perhaps with the Harpocrates from Taxila (p. 158), is the most noteworthy work of its kind from the East.

A little further north, at Akota in Baroda State, the bronze handle of a similar jug bearing a figure of Cupid (pl. XXVIA, B, p. 149) has been discovered recently during the excavation, by the Baroda University, of the ancient site of Ankottaka. It is closely comparable with the handle of the jug from Hoby (pl. II, p. 21) at the other end of the Roman map. From Karvan in the same state a cameo of exuberant sub-classical workmanship has also been recovered (pl. XXVIc, p. 149), but details are at present lacking.

Also from central India, generally from the territory of the Andhra empire, come a number of imitations of Roman coins, made locally as ornaments and mostly pierced or looped for suspension. They are normally of terracotta and were doubtless originally gilded. The most remarkable series was unearthed at the Andhra town of Kondapur in Hyderabad State and is preserved in the Hyderabad (Deccan) museum (pls. XXVIII, XXIX, pp. 156-7). It consists of at least 20 recognizable imitations of *aurei* or *denarii* of Tiberius (d. A.D. 37), with an Indianized version of the head of the emperor on the obverse and of Livia as Pax on the reverse. Both sides bear garbled inscriptions. Two similar clay *bullae*, one of them again imitating a Tiberius (with Livia-Pax facing the wrong way, as befits a copy), were found at the Chandravalli site already mentioned. Another, also of clay, was dug up on the Kolhapur mound, and yet others bearing romanized heads come from Ujjain and Sisupalgarh, and even from Rajghat on the outskirts of Benares, further north. A stone mould for casting a metal medallion of this class was found long ago at Besnagar, near Bhilsa in Gwalior State, and two gold medallions of sub-classical type and pierced for suspension were recovered at Nagarjunikonda in the Guntur district from a Buddhist *stūpa* ascribed to the 2nd-3rd centuries A.D. Another pierced gold imitation of an issue of Antoninus Pius was found with a pierced genuine *aureus* of Commodus at Chakerbedha, Bilaspur district, C.P. This list is not complete but sufficiently indicates the astonishing vogue of Roman coin-types over a large part of central India in the 1st and 2nd centuries.

At the same time be it emphasized that, for all the vigour of its impact, the Roman trade implied by these odds and ends had no appreciable or durable effect upon the cultures of the peninsula. It left a superficial imprint here and there, sometimes in remarkably remote places, but nowhere south of the Vindhyas was that imprint more than a graffito upon an essentially self-sufficient native fabric. Only when we move northwards towards the foot-hills of the Himalaya do we find evidences of a more significant and lasting penetration of Western ideas, and to this difficult problem we must now turn.

XIII · PAKISTAN AND AFGHANISTAN

UNLIKE the south, India north of the Vindhya Range produced no great quantity of goods of the kind demanded by the Mediterranean market. Cotton was grown there, and the carnelian of Rajpipla was doubtless in some request then as now. But it is primarily as a channel for trade in transit from remoter sources that north-western India comes into the present story. The *Periplus*, as we have seen, includes turquoise, lapis lazuli, 'Seric' skins and silk amongst the exports from the Indus delta, and these commodities have nothing in origin to do with the lands south of the Himalaya. Turquoise is above all a product of northern Iran; lapis lazuli comes from Badakshan, in the north-eastern corner of Afghanistan; the Seres, elsewhere associated with the silk and iron trade, are vaguely central or eastern Asiatic, and the skins described as Seric are evidently thought of as derived from High Asia; silk yarn was itself at this time a Chinese monopoly. For all these wares the direct passage to the West would have been the so-called Silk Route, across Iran to Syria. Astride this route, however, stood the implacable barrier of Parthia. Always in active rivalry and often at war with the Roman empire, Parthia blocked the Orient trade by extortionate levy or actual veto. The well-informed Chinese chronicles record that the Roman 'kings always desired to send embassies to China, but the An-hsi [Parthians] wished to carry on trade with them in Chinese silks and it is for this reason that they were cut off from communication'.[1] Thus save when on rare occasions a successful Roman campaign momentarily reopened the western sector of the Silk Route, this ceased to operate as a main artery of trade. It passed indeed out of Western knowledge; so much so that after Trajan's advance

[1] F. Hirth, *China and the Roman Orient* (Leipsic, etc., 1885), p. 42; F. J. Teggart, *Rome and China* (Univ. of California, 1939), p. 145.

to the Tigris early in the 2nd century it was found necessary to explore the route afresh, if, as seems likely, we should ascribe to this period the pioneer mission sent by a Macedonian merchant, one 'Maës called also Titianus' to the Stone Tower (Tashkurgan, between Yarkand and Badakshan) and thence to 'Sēra, the metropolis of the Seres'.[1]   With the journey of Julianus's knight to the Baltic (p. 9), this enterprise ranks amongst the great adventures of Roman commerce.

The Maës episode alone sufficiently emphasizes the normal insignificance of the main overland route through western Asia in Imperial times.   Whether or to what extent a route further north from the Oxus by way of the Caspian to the Black Sea was found more practicable we do not know. The Asiatic connections of the Greek cities of South Russia suggest the possibility of easier access along it, but evidence is at present lacking.   Alexandria at least is unlikely to have used it, and Alexandria was the focus of the Orient trade. Nor, in the light of the *Periplus* and of archaeology, is there room for doubt as to the main lines of Alexandrian traffic with central Asia and China.   They lay through West Pakistan and northern India, where geographical and political factors combined to facilitate them.

First, geography.   On the map, the Himalayan massif and its extensions give the Indian sub-continent an aspect of exclusiveness but are in fact penetrable at a number of points. For example, there are routes from China to the Brahmaputra in Assam, and it may have been along these routes that silk sometimes reached the coastal trade of the peninsula (p. 137).   Through Sikkim it is possible to reach India from the Tibetan plateau.   Further west a number of feasible if arduous routes enter Kashmir from Turkestan; the most notable of them used the famous Karakoram Pass, a desolate highway, if such it can be called, from High Asia into trans-Indus Kashmir.   But neither this nor any other of these northern approaches has played any dominant role in the

[1] Ptolemy, I, II, citing Marinus.

history of commerce. Their historical importance lay
rather in another context altogether, as occasional channels
for the diffusion of Buddhism from India to central Asia and
China. The main entries lay on the north-western frontier
of what is now Pakistan, and converge on the plain of
Peshawar, using at first the line of the Kabul river and, from
the 2nd century A.D., the Khyber Pass.

Through these north-western gaps penetrated one of the
great trade-routes of ancient Asia. It left the east-west
trans-Asian Silk Route at Balkh, the little village which
to-day represents Bactra, Mother of Cities, once a vast
metropolis seven miles in circuit. Balkh lies on the steppe of
Afghan Turkestan some 20 miles south of the Oxus, outside
the former frontier of Parthia, and was a nodal point in
the Asian traffic system. From it the old branch-route strikes
south-eastwards to the Kabul river and India through clefts
in the Hindu-Kush, thus circumventing the more formidable
mountain-barriers further east. However devious, this is in
fact the easiest highway from central Asia to north-western
India. From China, says the *Periplus*, 'raw silk and silk
yarn and silk cloth are brought on foot through Bactria to
Barygaza'.

Secondly, the political factors. In the latter part of the
1st century the route just mentioned was adopted as the axis
of advance by central Asian hordes under the leadership of
one of their septs, the Kushans, who had overrun Bactria
and now overflowed into India. The chronology of the
Kushāna empire is still in dispute, but by the beginning of the
2nd century A.D., if not earlier, it extended to the mouths of
the Indus and far into the north Indian plains, thus unifying
the political control of a vast tract of country from the
Hindu-Kush to the sea and so, incidentally, simplifying and
reducing Customs dues. Unlike their Parthian contem-
poraries, the Kushāna kings were singularly catholic in their
political and cultural outlook and modelled their gold
coinage (p. 142)—perhaps even some part of their religion—
on that of the Roman West. There can be no doubt that

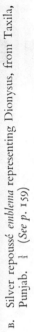
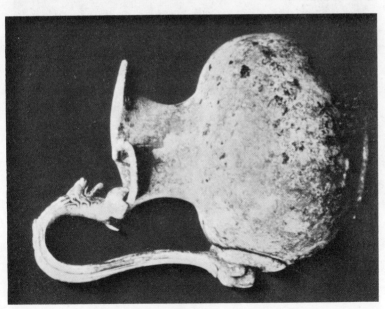

A. Bronze jug from Kolhapur, Western India. ½ (*See p.* 151)

B. Silver repoussé *emblema* representing Dionysus, from Taxila, Punjab. ¼ (*See p.* 150)

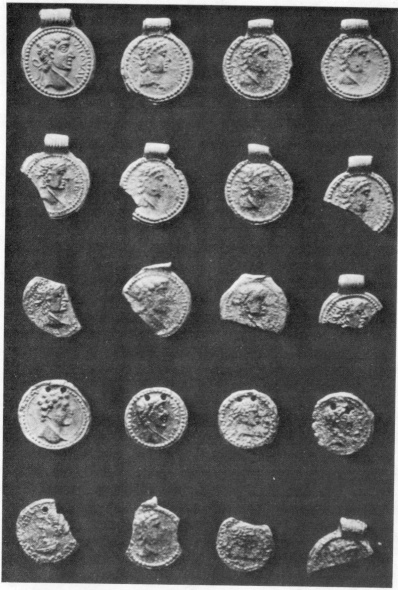

Terracotta imitations of coins of Tiberius (obverses), from Kondapur,
Hyderabad State.   Nearly ¼

(*See p.* 152)

Terracotta imitations of coins of Tiberius (reverses), from Kondapur,
Hyderabad State.   Nearly ¼
(*See p.* 152)

Air-view of part of Taxila (Sirkap), Punjab, as excavated. (*See p.* 158)

the Western trade which passed through their territory was directly fostered by them. To that trade we must now return.

Be it repeated at the outset that, greatly simplified, the route followed by this east Asian trade was as follows (*end map*). From the Chinese province of Honan or thereabouts, tracks converged upon the upper valley of the Hwang Ho and thence proceeded by alternative courses, which do not concern us here, to Kashgar and Tashkurgan on the flank of the Pamirs, and so by the Oxus valley to Bactra. At Bactra the route divided in the fashion already indicated. Political conditions permitting, the traveller could continue westwards by way of Rhagae (Tehran) to Seleucia or Antioch. On the other hand, he could turn sharply south-eastwards to Pakistan and India, passing a number of trade-route cities of which Begram, 45 miles north of Kabul, and Taxila, on the borders of the Punjab and the North-West Frontier province of Pakistan, are for our present purpose the most important. From this sector the valleys of the Indus and its tributaries offered approaches to the Arabian Sea; or the journey could be continued, roughly along the line of the Grand Trunk Road, to the Kushāna capital of Mathura (Muttra), south of Delhi, and thence south-westwards through Ujjain to the port of Barygaza or Broach.

Many sites along this immense track-system must be capable of producing relevant evidence, but only two of them—those just mentioned—have been sufficiently explored to throw any considerable light upon the extent and character of the Western trade. Something must be said of each of them.

For more than twenty years Taxila has been submitted to large-scale excavation, and the results have been lavishly published.[1] Here it will suffice to observe that in the 1st century A.D. it was a walled city, now known as Sirkap, three-quarters of a mile in length, designed to include an

[1] J. Marshall, *Taxila* (Cambridge, 3 vols., 1951).

acropolis on an intrusive, rocky headland, and a 'lower town' laid out in regular blocks or *insulae* on what may fairly be described as the Hellenistic pattern (pl. XXX, p. 157). It was at first under Parthian rulers who seem to have owed no allegiance to the central Parthian power in Iran; but soon after the middle of the century it passed to the Kushans and was, perhaps a century later, rebuilt by them a mile away to the north (now Sirsukh). Of the new foundation we have little knowledge, but it was the Sirkap city that straddled the period of the *Periplus*.

Comparison with the contemporary town of Arikamedu in the far south is at once inevitable and instructive. At Arikamedu, it may be recalled that a few months' excavation revealed a considerable mass of Mediterranean pottery—wine-jars, table-ware, lamps, even gems and glass. Many years of excavation at Taxila have yielded only a single wine-jar, three or four fragments of Western glass (fig. 19, 3), a gem or two, but not even a scrap of Arretine table-ware, not a single Roman lamp.[1] The contrast is significant. There was at Taxila, unlike Arikamedu, no terminal trade in the usual Mediterranean commodities, wine and crockery. On the other hand, there were other contacts with the West, of a kind which had in fact, as we shall see, a far more enduring influence upon Asian thought or expression. Notable amongst these evidences is a charming bronze statuette of the child-god Harpocrates, his right forefinger raised to his lips possibly in a gesture of silence (*frontispiece*). On his head are the Egyptian crowns of the north and the south and, since the cult was centred upon Alexandria, the figure is likely to have come from there, in or about the 1st century A.D. A similar statuette will be noted from the Begram hoard (p. 164).

[1] From this generalization I exclude a few sherds showing Hellenizing features in fabric or decoration which probably represent infiltration from western Asia, but have nothing to do with the Italic imports of the main body of Augustan and post-Augustan trade. The so-called 'Greek black ware' from Taxila is a widespread North-Indian fabric, most if not all of which was doubtless made in India itself.

Other bronze and gold statuettes or reliefs from the site, such as a Cupid and a 'Venus', have been claimed as Graeco-Roman and owe something to Western influence but are probably of Indian manufacture. On the other hand, a silver repoussé *emblema* or circular decoration, representing

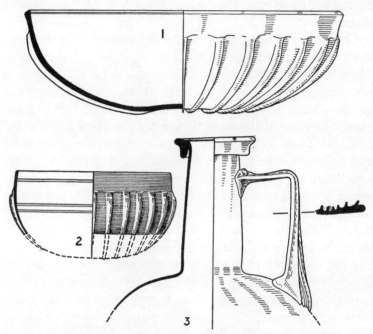

Fig. 19   Roman glass: 1, from Begram, Afganistan; 2, from Arikamedu, S. India; 3, from Taxila (Sirkap), W. Pakistan. $\frac{1}{3}$

Dionysus or Silenus, is a somewhat crude piece of Western workmanship (pl. XXVIIb, p. 156); it is probably from the centre of a dish, but, when lost, was mounted on a silver stand as a table ornament. With it was found a silver spoon with rat-tail ridge and cloven-hoof handle of Graeco-Roman type. Two or three bronze saucepans having tubular handles with ram's-head terminals are of similar derivation and are dated to the 1st century A.D. (again compare Begram, p. 164). Of the gems, two at least are imports from the Roman world: a gold-set carnelian bearing figures of Eros and Psyche with a small child, and a nicolo engraved with a winged cupid running after a bird and closely comparable with a gem from Arikamedu (p. 146). A *denarius* of Tiberius is also recorded, but otherwise Roman coinage is absent. A famous series of circular stone toilette trays show Western elements in their carved figure-groups, but are generally of Oriental workmanship.

These very various imports and derivatives tell a different story from the straightforward merchandise of the south. They hint at the casual acquisition of Western things; at opportunist purchase or levy from passing caravans carrying goods which may be broadly described as of the 'luxury' class. In view of the huge total extent of the material now available from Taxila, they do not suggest the purposeful and regular marketing of Mediterranean wares there. This conclusion will be discussed further at a later stage. Meanwhile, there is another aspect of the matter which must be touched upon in summary fashion.

An outstanding feature of the material recovered from Taxila and its environs is a considerable quantity of sculpture, in relief and in the round, in stone, clay and, above all, stucco. If we set aside the innumerable small terracottas as secondary commercial products, the more monumental residue is still impressive in bulk, range, and sometimes quality. Most of it is derived from Buddhist shrines and monasteries; works of a definitely secular origin scarcely occur. More will be said at a later stage of the general problem which it raises. Meanwhile, examples of this art are cited to illustrate a specific character of some part of it—namely, a recurrent Western, Graeco-Roman element of a striking and significant kind.

The first is the stucco head of a smiling child (pl. XXXIA, p. 164) from the monastery of Jaulian near Taxila. The head would be in place on any Graeco-Roman site, and has nothing in origin to do with the art of India. A similar comment is applicable to the stucco head of a fawn or satyr (pl. XXXIB, p. 164) with pointed ears and snub nose, from the apsidal temple beside the main street of Sirkap (visible in pl. XXX, p. 157). Again the type is purely classical. A third example of the kind is the beautiful life-size stucco head of a youth from the Dhamarajika monastery at Taxila (pl. XXXIIA, pp. 164-5). The head is unmistakably reminiscent of 2nd-century Roman portraits, such as that of the youthful Marcus Aurelius in the Capitoline Museum at Rome. Other Westernizing examples might be cited from Taxila, together with several in which the Western element is combined with Indian traits. Amongst the latter is a schist frieze from the Kunala monastery at Sirkap, showing *putti* and other figures amidst the serpentine loops of a continuous wreath with pendant grape-clusters pecked by birds. This classical motif—a recurrent one in north-western India at the period—shows, by the fleshiness of the figures and by some of the postures, the hand of the Indian carver, but is otherwise a non-Indian conception (pl. XXXIII, pp. 164-5).

Outside Taxila, within the North-West Frontier Province of what is now West Pakistan and in adjacent Afghanistan, such Westernizing work is a familiar phenomenon. Thus from Charsada, on the Peshawar plain, comes a terracotta version of the Apollo Belvedere (pl. XXXIIB, pp. 164-5), and from the same region is recorded a stone relief representing Laocoön, in Western costume, in the act of prodding the Trojan Horse, with a very Indian Cassandra in the background: a strange and revealing mixture of India and the Mediterranean with a distinctively Western theme (pl. XXXIV, p. 165). And again a stucco head of a warrior, also from the Peshawar district, recalls the typical Gaul of Roman art, whilst at the Buddhist site of Hadda in Afghanistan a reflection of the 'Antinous' type of 2nd-century Rome is recognizable in the stucco figure of an effeminate youth, now at the Musée Guimet in Paris.

To these interchanges and resemblances between West and East we shall return. Before doing so, however, we must glance at another site, famous in consequence of its partial excavation by the French Archaeological Mission to

Afghanistan between 1936 and 1942, under the direction successively of J. Hackin and R. Ghirshman.[1]

Some 45 miles north of Kabul, at the junction of the rivers Ghorband and Panjshir beneath the towering range of the Hindu-Kush, are the remains of an ancient town now known as Begram, but formerly, as it seems, the Kapisi, royal capital of Kapisa, visited by the Chinese Buddhist pilgrim Hiuan-tsang in A.D. 644. It lies, as already mentioned, beside the branch-route from Bactra to India. The site itself falls topographically into three parts. Dominating the actual confluence is an area of about 150×100 yards known as the Bordj-i-'Abdullah or alternatively as 'the Ancient Royal Town', fortified by an earthen rampart revetted externally and internally with unbaked brick. Inadequate excavation has suggested that this may be the work of Graeco-Bactrian kings of the 2nd century B.C. About 350 yards to the south, at the head of a gentler rise, is another oblong fortified area, 280×80 yards in extent, known as 'the New Royal Town'. The slope between the two enclosures also had lateral defences, but is unexplored.

Present interest centres upon the New Royal Town, where three main phases of occupation, ranging from the 1st or 2nd century B.C. to the 5th A.D., have been identified. The first phase dates, perhaps, from the Indo-Greek kings, and to it belong stalwart fortifications of unbaked brick on stone footings, with rectangular salients or towers at frequent intervals and two ditches. On the southern side was a central gate which has not been planned. Within there is a hint, but no more, of a rectilinear lay-out as at Taxila (Sirkap). The phase was succeeded without visible break by Phase 2, ascribed to the great Kanishka in the second quarter of the 2nd century. The new régime was marked by fresh build-ings and repairs to old ones and, in particular, included a

---

[1] J. Hackin, *Recherches archéologiques à Begram* (Mémoires de la Délégation Archéologique Française en Afghanistan, IX, 1939); R. Ghirshman, *Bégram, Recherches archéologiques et historiques sur les Kouchans* (Cairo, L'Institut Français d'Archéologie Orientale, 1946).

'palace' of which more will be said presently. Ghirshman has made a good case for ending the second phase with the conquest of the territory by the Sasanid king Shapur I about A.D. 250, basing his conclusion upon evidences of violent destruction, coins, and a tomb-inscription at Naqsh-i-Rustam near Persepolis in Iran, which indicates that Shapur extended his empire to the Indus. After a brief interim, the city was partially rebuilt and, so far as excavated, appears to have been destroyed finally by the White Huns after A.D. 450. The whereabouts of the town visited by Hiuan-tsang two centuries later has not been ascertained.

Two rooms in the 'palace' of the second phase produced a hoard of Mediterranean and Oriental wares the like of which has not been seen elsewhere in Asia. At least one of the doors had been blocked up anciently, and there is no doubt that the objects had been carefully stored and were not in actual use at the time of the destruction. Thus in the north-western quarter of one of the rooms were placed glass vessels from Syria or Egypt, whilst in the centre and southern part were coffers and plaques of carved bone and ivory from India. Elsewhere was a group of bronze bowls from Western factories, and a cluster of steelyard-weights in the form of Minerva or Mars (pl. XXXVA, p. 168). Elsewhere again were the remains of lacquer bowls from China. From the ends of the earth—from the West, from the Far East, from India—exotic things of beauty and worth had been gathered into the few square yards of these two sealed rooms, as so much bullion into a bank strong-room.

Associated Kushāna coins, including at least one of Kanishka himself and ending with the last king of the 'second Kushāna dynasty', Vasudeva, indicate the general period covered by the assemblage—namely, the 2nd century A.D. and the earlier half of the 3rd. The component parts, and in particular the Western glass which ranges in type from the (end of the) 1st (fig. 19, 1) to the 3rd centuries, tally. In other words, the hoard is not an integral deposit, but an accumulation representing about 150 years. The easiest explanation is doubtless the correct one. The store was probably a Customs depot for the receipt of dues in kind collected by the kings or viceroys of Kapisa from the caravans which traversed the adjacent highway in the luxury traffic of Orient and Occident.

Let us for a moment glance at some of those wares which concern our special study. Statuettes of bronze include a little Harpocrates similar to that already described from Taxila and, like it, presumably from Alexandria;[1] a Hercules crowned with the Egyptian calathus and probably of similar origin (pl. XXXVB, p. 168); a rider in classical garb (pl. XXXVI, pp. 168-9); and a grotesque 'philosopher' of the low-comedy type of which there are many examples in minor Roman art. The steelyard-weights in the form of classical busts have already been mentioned. Bronze feet from stands for lamps or incense or from caskets represent normal Western furniture; and bronze bowls identical with some of those which penetrated into Free Germany occurred here also in considerable quantity. Alabaster jugs and 'saucepans', the latter with ram's-head handle, are classical copies of normal metal forms. The glass includes a great number of familiar types, from the universal 'pillared' bowl of the 1st or early 2nd century to a fine bowl of millefiori also of early date, a vase with a representation of ships and a lighthouse (tentatively identified by H. Seyrig with the pharos of Alexandria), painted and cut-glass goblets (pl. XXXVII, pp. 168-9), and vessels with semi-detached network sur-round. But most surprising in this remote spot is a number of plaster medallions, 6-8 in. in diameter, bearing Mediterranean reliefs representing Minerva and other classical subjects, such as the vine harvest or Eros and Psyche, of a kind well known in the classical world (pl. XXXVIII, p. 169). Such medallions were used as models by metal-workers, who transferred them to the silver dishes for which Alexandria and other Graeco-Roman centres were famous. Alexandria

[1] P. 158. The Begram Harpocrates, now in the Kabul Museum, had had the right arm wrongly affixed when I saw it in 1946.

B. Stucco head of a satyr, from Taxila, Punjab. ½
(*See p.* 160)

A. Stucco head of an infant, from Taxila, Punjab. ¾
(*See p.* 160)

XXXII

B. Terracotta head based on the Apollo Belvedere, from Charsada,
N.-W. (Frontier Province, 1. (See p. 161)

A. Stucco head of a youth, from Taxila, Punjab. ⅓
(See p. 161)

Stone frieze from Taxila, Punjab.   Length 15 in.
(*See p. 161*)

Stone relief showing Laocoön and the Trojan Horse, from the North-West Frontier Province. $\frac{1}{6}$

(*See p. 161*)

had special cause to use her vast local resources of plaster, and further reference will be made to the wider significance of this fact. If in regarding the Begram hoard we ignore the astonishing beauty of the great collection of carved ivory from India or the crumbling remains of lacquerwork from China, and look only at these and other products of Roman Imperial craftsmanship, the spectacle, whether in the Kabul Museum or in the Musée Guimet in Paris, where a part of the collection can be seen, is one which stirs the imagination. And derelict Begram itself, where so little work has yet been done though with such dramatic result, remains a challenge to the explorer.

And now for certain wider issues. If one were asked to name the most penetrating and enduring impact of the Roman upon the Eastern world, the answer could scarcely be in doubt. In the early centuries of the present era the Buddhist art of north-western India and Afghanistan absorbed Western modes of expression, varying in kind and degree from instance to instance and from mind to critical mind, but constituting in the aggregate one of the most notorious and intriguing problems of art-history. Nor is the matter exclusively one of fashions and formulae. Eastern religious thought was itself undergoing at this time a process of change which presented significant analogies with the contemporary developments of Western metaphysics. The Western imperialistic idea and the Eurasian mysticism in which it was ultimately enveloped had appreciably close counterparts in the Orient; so much so that a good deal of nonsense has been written about the supposed interrelationship of Christianity and Buddhism, and may serve to warn us against an excessive affiliation of the respective arts. The main facts, however, are sufficiently clear. East and West were moving vaguely in the same direction, they had something of the same spiritual and aesthetic needs. Given the opportunity, there was every reason for a certain interchange or borrowing of material expression. And since

M

1870, when an official of the Punjab service brought to England from north-western India a small collection of 'Indo-Scythian' sculptures, it has been recognized that in and about the plain of Peshawar—the ancient Gandhara—and thence far afield in Asia a whole complex of Western ideas was in fact drawn at this time into the service of Buddhism.

Gandhara art, and that far wider art-province of which Gandhara provided a regional facet, does not concern us here in any detail. Its literature is immense and growing. The absence of an objective chronology has facilitated an infinite manipulation of the evidence in accordance with taste and theory, and until modern methods of excavation are applied to Buddhist sites far more rigidly than they have been in the past this source of doubt and disputation will remain.

Meanwhile, the governing principle may be emphasized that, with stray exceptions, this Romano-Indian art was confined to Buddhist patronage. Not only did the Buddhism of the age and place supply the religious and aesthetic context, but it also supplied the necessary wealth and backing. From the arrival of the Kushan dynasty in the latter half of the 1st century to the devastation of the whole region by the White Huns in the latter half of the 5th, Buddhism went from strength to strength, Buddhist monasteries multiplied across the landscape, and within the individual convents sculptured dedications jostled one another in ever-growing mass about the central shrine. For an understanding of this tumultuous manifestation a word or two must be said about the controlling faith.

Buddhism was in origin not a religion, but a philosophy of life. The Buddha, the Enlightened One, was not a god; he was an inspired teacher who, about 500 B.C., preached on the Ganges plains the Middle Path between indulgence and asceticism and sought an ultimate deliverance from accumulated sin in supreme detachment, *nirvana*. Later, however, by a process of evolution natural to a land where the teacher has always been revered, the Buddha was increasingly regarded as a divine Being to whom prayer might be offered. The earlier type of Buddhism is commonly distinguished as that of the *Hinayana* persuasion or the Buddhism of the Lesser Vehicle, and the later type (which did not wholly supersede the other) as that of the *Mahayana* persuasion or the Greater Vehicle. The latter persuasion reached maturity in and about the time of King Kanishka, who is now widely thought to have flourished in the second quarter of the 2nd century A.D., about the time of Hadrian and Antoninus Pius in the West.

In artistic expression the outstanding difference between these two main types of Buddhism was that during the prevalence of the *Hinayana* teaching the Buddha himself was never represented. His presence was symbolized by a chair, a footprint, an umbrella, a riderless horse. About this symbol crowd the other participants in the scene, but there is no central commanding figure. In *Mahayana* Buddhism, on the other hand, the figure of the divine Buddha controls the assembly and is the focus of its composition. Both iconographically and aesthetically the change was revolutionary.

Artistically, this change found its first full expression in what is now West Pakistan and Afghanistan. The new Buddhism, amongst other faiths, received the patronage of the liberal-minded Kanishka, and the wealth of the Kushan empire provided a suitable environment for its development. What was lacking was any comprehensive traditional idiom in which to express the new observance; and it was here that Western art, already sufficiently familiar from the Western luxury trade described above—if not from the actual importation of Western craftsmen (p. 133)—came to the rescue. In the Roman Imperial West, the figure of the Roman emperor was established as the dominant feature of an artistic composition. Now, both this and some of its accessories and details, with others from Roman heroic and funerary art, were adapted to the Buddhist problem.

Figures clad in Western clothing,[1] Western types such as *putti* or *erotes* and garlands, satyrs, Apollos, Minervas, even an occasional scene from Western legend such as that of the Trojan horse, and Western grouping such as that associated with the state arrival or departure of the Roman emperor, found their way into the sculptors' workshops of Gandhara and the adjacent region of Afghanistan. There they were to a greater or less extent transmuted by the Buddhist craftsman and given a Buddhist context. The fact that the region had previously been ruled by Indo-Greek kings may have, in some small degree, prepared the way for this influx. But it seems certain that, for more than two centuries before the Mahayana persuasion and its art took shape, the surviving Hellenism of Bactra had dwindled to vanishing point, and the most that it can have bequeathed to the subjects of Kanishka was a faint surviving sympathy for Western things. The idiom or 'language' of the new Buddhist art, in so far as it was non-native, was bred from new contacts. It was essentially a cultural by-product of the Kushana commerce which brought into and through the kingdom objects and craftsmanship of the Roman empire.

As examples from Taxila have indicated, this Buddhist art has survived mainly in sculptural form, partly in stone, partly in stucco or plaster, and partly in clay. Most of the stone sculpture is carved in a green schist from the periphery of the ancient Gandhara. Its comparatively high 'survival value' and portability have tended to concentrate attention upon it and perhaps to exaggerate its relative importance. Far more widely spread in space, and probably in time, is the equivalent sculpture in painted stucco or clay, which is found not only in Gandhara, but far afield along the arterial routes that Buddhist monks shared with the traders through the

[1] The least Western of these figures is often the much-discussed figure of the Buddha himself. His monk's robe occasionally bears a more or less remote resemblance to the toga, but this resemblance is commonly exaggerated by modern writers, whilst the head is in most instances completely Oriental. It is in the details and grouping of subsidiary figures that Western iconography is more liable to intrude.

B. Bronze statuette of Hercules wearing the *calathus*, from the Begram hoard. $\frac{1}{2}$ (*See p.* 164)

A. Bronze steelyard weight, from the Begram hoard, Afghanistan. $\frac{3}{4}$ (*See p.* 163)

Bronze figurine of armed horseman, from the Begram hoard. ⅓
(*See p.* 164)

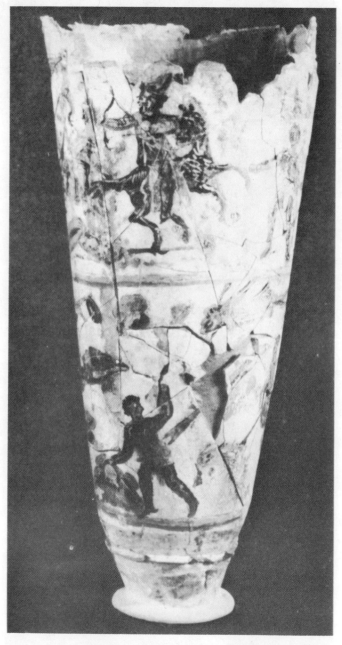

Roman glass beaker with painted decoration, from
the Begram hoard. ⅟₁ (*See p.* 164)

Stucco *emblemata* representing the grape-harvest (below) and
Athena (above) from the Begram hoard. $\frac{3}{4}$ (*See p.* 164)

Hindu-Kush and the Turkestans, along the China road. In Afghanistan the best-known source for this sculpture, mostly in stucco, but sometimes in stone, is Hadda, near Jalalabad, where there was a large Buddhist monastic settlement, but another monastery as far north as Kunduz on the Turkestan steppe in the same country has produced similar stuccoes, others are known in central Asia, and in the opposite direction stucco fragments have been found at Mohenjo-daro in Sind. It is observable that the stucco-medium, by reason of its easy manipulation, is associated with a greater range and vividness of expression than the stonework; and, on the other hand, that this facility, and the possibility of using moulds, encouraged mass production, particularly in the later and more decadent phases, when the use of the more laborious stone may have died out.

For the dating of this art there is little evidence. The earliest undisputed representations of the Buddha are those on certain gold coins of Kanishka, about or a little before A.D. 150, and this date accords well with what we know of the development of the Mahayana observance. A terminal date for the bulk of the surviving material in and about Gandhara is more securely fixed by the havoc wrought by the White Huns there during the half-century following A.D. 450. At Taxila a considerable quantity of stucco sculpture has been found in position in monasteries destroyed at that time and gives us a consistent picture of the condition of the art about the middle of the 5th century. We see that it was then highly stylized, but still retained traces of its dual (Eastern and Western) origin. The main brackets for this classicizing art in its homeland may be provisionally stated therefore as A.D. 100 and 450, though the tradition is still recognizable long after this period and in regions as remote as South India and the fringes of the Gobi Desert.

It remains to consider these various facts and probabilities in the general context of time and place. How did the Western elements reach the Gandhara studios? A part of the answer has been already given by Taxila and Begram.

Behind the Western statuettes, glass and stuccoes from those sites loom the presence and personality of Alexandria. Other Western workshops, notably those of Syria, doubtless contributed; but the dominance of Alexandria is scarcely in doubt. Long ago, before most of these discoveries were made, Rostovtzeff was able to affirm that 'the active agents in the exchange of goods between the Roman Empire and China were the Alexandrian merchants. Without them the commerce with India would probably not have existed.' More recently a growing knowledge of the art and craftsmanship of Palmyra has pointed to a certain affinity of Palmyrene textiles and jewellery with those of India, and occasionally to comparable traits, which may or may not be significant, between Palmyrene and Gandhara sculpture.[1] Such resemblances arise naturally from the known trade-connections of Palmyra with the Orient, but they merely supplement the arterial traffic of Alexandria. Above all, Alexandria was the principal home of stucco sculpture in the West. Adjoining the city for miles the coastline is white with the gypsum which is the raw material of stucco. And when in Ptolemaic and Roman times (from the 3rd century B.C. forwards) statuary was demanded at Alexandria in conformity with Greek and Roman taste, the cheap local stucco was extensively used as a substitute for the relatively costly white marble which had to be imported from considerable distances. There can be little doubt that it was the Alexandrian trade with and through the Kushan empire that carried thither, not merely goods and ideas, but also the stucco-technique; and that thereafter the use of this mobile medium spread rapidly with the Buddhist monachism that travelled northwards and eastwards with the caravans as far as the border of China.

A rich and dominantly Alexandrian trade and a peculiarly receptive environment were, then, contributory factors in

[1] H. Seyrig, 'Ornamenta Palmyrena Antiquiora', in *Syria*, XXI (1940), 305ff.; Rostovtzeff, *Revue des Arts Asiatiques*, VII (1931-32), 209; A. C. Soper, 'The Roman Style in Gandhara', in *American Journ. of Archaeology*, LV (1951), 311.

the making of Romano-Buddhist art. It may be doubted, however, whether they operated without a third medium. Before A.D. 100 India was in intermittent diplomatic contact with the West—through the various missions to which reference has been made (p. 133), and, by fair assumption, through others unrecorded—and was actually employing Western craftsmen. The ancient story that King Gondophernes purchased St. Thomas as a slave in Jerusalem for the purpose of building his palace at Taxila may not be true, but must have been sufficiently possible to achieve acceptance; and more historical references to the reputation enjoyed by Yavana craftsmen employed in India are impressively numerous.[1] The suggestion that, on analogy, an occasional Western sculptor was similarly employed in Gandhara for training and assisting local craftsmen at a time of unprecedented demand is entirely consistent with this trend, and indeed completes the picture.

In summary, therefore, the basic explanation of Romano-Buddhist art in north-western India appears to be threefold. First, there were the new and congenial requirements of a *Mahayana* Buddhism backed by powerful patronage. Secondly, there was close commercial contact in high-grade wares, including sculpture in bronze and stucco, with the West and, in particular, with Alexandria. Thirdly, there is analogy for the direct employment of small numbers of Western craftsman *in partibus*. To these factors may be added a fourth contributory factor in the incidental importation from Alexandria of a technique, that of stucco sculpture, which lent itself in a welcome measure to easy diffusion and mass-production. There the problem in its present limited setting may be left.

[1] See above, p. 133, and A. C. Soper, as cited, p. 305.

XIV · THE FAR EAST

THE author of the *Periplus* was aware of lands beyond India, but knew almost nothing of them. East of the Ganges lay Chrysē, the Golden, 'the very last land toward the east'. Northwards was This, a land 'hard of access', with a great inland city called Thinae, whence silk was brought on the one hand to Bactria and Barygaza and on the other hand to the Ganges and South India. A century later, Ptolemy was able to collect extensive lists of place-names from the coasts, islands and hinterland of these parts, but had little knowledge of their interrelationship. He was indeed misled by a basic conception that the Indian Ocean was a larger Mediterranean, south-eastern Asia being twisted southwards and westwards to join the coast of Africa somewhere south of Zanzibar. In the circumstances, it is not very profitable to spend time on an attempted reconciliation of his data with fact. His 'Golden Chersonese', like the Chrysē of the *Periplus*, may be equated with Burma and Malaya, and his 'Great Gulf' was probably the Gulf of Siam. In the Golden Chersonese he notes amongst other places two markets or *emporia*, Takola and Sabana, of which the former has been placed tentatively in the neighbourhood of Rangoon, where there is said to be some evidence of a place called Takkhala, Takola or Tagala in the middle ages.[1] But only archaeological evidence can now give substance to identifications of this vague kind, and such evidence has scarcely been sought. That tangible evidence does in fact await discovery is suggested by the preliminary excavation of an ancient town-site known as Oc-eo, 15 miles from the shores of the Gulf of Siam, in Indo-China.

The site of Oc-eo lies by the delta of the Mekong river,

[1] On this point, and generally, see J. W. McCrindle, 'Ptolemy's Geography of India and Southern Asia', in *The Indian Antiquary* XIII (Bombay, 1884), 372, etc.; and McCrindle, *Ancient India as described by Ptolemy* (Calcutta, 1927).

on the fringe of the province of Long-xuyen, and is a complex of low mounds rising from the alluvial plain. The remains are those of a town framed by buried defences which form an oblong of rather more than 3,000 by 1,500 yards, with the considerable area of about two square miles. This area seems to have included timber huts (possibly on piles), and brick and stone buildings, together with rice-fields. Excavations were begun here in 1944 by M. L. Malleret on behalf of the École Française d' Extrême-Orient,[1] but have been curtailed by war conditions.

The excavator found remains of rectangular structures with flat roof-tiles, and more or less completely excavated two of them. One, of brick, consisted largely of closed cells which may (I suggest) have constituted the podium of a temple, comparable with the cellular podia characteristic of waterlogged sites of 7th century and earlier temples in Pakistan and northern India.[2] The other structure, of brick and granite, was identified as a *mandapa* or temple building with terracotta plaques bearing floral decoration and heads of monsters of a characteristically Indian type. Immediately flanking it were slight remains of two annexes, in one of which was part of a stone statuette of the Hindu god Vishnu. Other objects found during the excavations included relics of the cults of Siva, Vishnu and Surya, traces of gold-, iron- and copper-working, many thousands of beads of semi-precious stones, cameos of carnelian, crystal or jasper bearing in some cases brief Brahmi inscriptions of the 2nd-5th centuries A.D., fragments of bronze figurines, amongst which are noted Buddhist representations, a head and image in the Gandhara style and a statuette recalling the art of Amaravati, gold jewellery, and a wide range of terracotta ornaments. As a whole, the culture is half-native, half-Indian, and is appropriate to its peninsular location. But

[1] Preliminary report in *Bulletin de l'École Française d'Extrême-Orient* XLV, fasc. I (Paris, 1951), 75ff., with other references.

[2] R. E. M. Wheeler, *Five Thousand Years of Pakistan* (London, 1950), pp. 102-3.

with these Indian elements are a number of objects or influences from further afield. Thus a blue glass gem bears in intaglio a bearded head with plaited hair and a Phrygian cap, probably of Sasanian origin. Other gems are regarded by the excavator as Roman: one bearing a cock on a chariot drawn by two mice, others with *grylli* or composite animals of a kind familiar in Roman art, others again with busts of Roman or romanizing type. A few of the beads are described as 'pseudo-Roman', but publication of them is awaited. No doubt at least attaches to a pierced gold coin of Antoninus Pius, dated to A.D. 152, and a second, less legible, of Marcus Aurelius.

All these Western elements should doubtless be ascribed to infiltration through India rather than to any more direct contact with the West. Nevertheless, it is a noteworthy coincidence that to the time of Marcus Aurelius the *Han Annals* attribute the arrival of an embassy from 'An-tun' (Marcus Aurelius Antoninus) at the Chinese court and the first opening up of intercourse with Ta-ts'in or the Roman Empire. The entry is as follows: 'They [the Romans] make coins of gold and silver. . . . They traffic by sea with An-hsi [Parthia] and T'ien-chu [India], the profit of which trade is tenfold. They are honest in their transactions, and there are no double prices. . . . The budget is based on a well-filled treasury. . . . Their kings always desired to send embassies to China, but the An-hsi [Parthians] wished to carry on trade with them in Chinese silks, and it is for this reason that they were cut off from communication. This lasted till the ninth year of the Yen-hsi period during the Emperor Huan-ti's reign [= A.D. 166] when the king of Ta-ts'in, An-tun, sent an embassy which, from the frontier of Jih-nan [Annam], offered ivory, rhinoceros horns and tortoiseshell. From that time dates the intercourse with this country.'[1] The *Annals* proceed to comment on the absence of jewels from the list of gifts offered by the 'embassy', and the comparative poverty

[1] F. Hirth, *China and the Roman Orient* (Leipsic, Munich, Shanghai and Hongkong, 1885), p. 42.

of the tribute does in fact suggest the opportunism of some private merchant rather than a considered Imperial mission. Nevertheless, the episode, which is thoroughly circumstantial in its attendant details and is unlikely to have been invented, is a further example of the adventurous spirit in which Roman trade was conducted *in partibus*.

For the rest, Roman or sub-Roman wares, particularly glass, have been found from time to time in China. In south-eastern Korea two of the mounds which mark the burials of the kings of the local kingdom of Silla, broadly bracketed between 100 B.C. and A.D. 600, have produced glass vessels which may be Roman of the 3rd or 4th century A.D. A glass dish, probably Roman, of about the same period is more vaguely recorded from Honan[1] and other early glass from China may include Western elements, though much more archaeological and spectrographic analysis is required before the extent of these elements can be estimated. If we accept the evidence of the *Pei-shih*, a relatively late version of earlier material, glass was not actually made in China until the second quarter of the 5th century A.D., when the process is said to have been introduced by traders from the country of Ta-yuch-chih, bordering on the north-west of India. Another version has it that the traders came from India itself. On the other hand it has been urged that certain Chinese glass beads resembling Western 'eye-beads', with the glass body inlaid with white rings and a coloured centre, indicate a partial introduction of the technique at a somewhat earlier date. Glass fragments found by Sir Aurel Stein in central Asia may indicate the line of approach, but once more the absence of precise detail is baffling. When China is once more accessible the whole problem is deserving of further attention. Meanwhile Rome in China remains the province of history— particularly of Chinese history—rather than of archaeology.

[1] For these and other Western objects from China, the most accessible source is C. G. Seligman, 'The Roman Orient and the Far East', in *Antiquity*, XI (1937), 5ff.

XV · RETROSPECT

ROMAN trade, diplomacy and 'drift' have now been traced, in however sketchy a fashion, far beyond the Imperial frontiers in Europe, Africa and Asia. No attempt has been made to re-traverse in detail the ground covered in the recent past by Charlesworth, Warmington or Eggers; on their basic work, and on their ancient authorities, the present book is founded. But here and there it has been possible to add to their material, to give it perhaps a new actuality and a new perspective. The French discoveries in Afghanistan and Indo-China, those of the British at Taxila and Arikamedu or of the Italians in the Fezzan, have necessitated a partial rewriting of the story. Only in Europe itself, to-day harassed and sub-divided, has discovery almost ceased for the time being.

In conclusion, let us glance at the evidence as a whole and estimate very briefly the value of the new material. Roman trafficking with lands outside the Empire was founded primarily on the supply of five commodities which were woven into the fabric of Imperial culture, and were essential in one way or another to the Imperial way of life. Free Germany produced the amber which was already an integral part of the equipment of southern Europe before the Empire was born. From tropical Africa came the ivory of infinite domestic use, either across the Sahara or by way of the Red Sea. Southern Arabia yielded the frankincense which had long been sought by the Pharaohs and the Achaemenids and, with gold and myrrh, was offered at Bethlehem. In peninsular India grows the abundant pepper which has for more than 2,000 years mitigated the cooking of the Western World. And China had a monopoly of silk until the 6th century A.D. Amber, ivory, incense, pepper, silk were the mainsprings of Roman long-range trade. The principal routes and markets were determined by them; a map of them is substantially a map of Imperial commerce as a whole. Into these routes and markets were fed, as was inevitable, a miscellany of other goods—pearls, semi-precious stones, tortoiseshell, muslin, skins, spices—which varied from place to place and served to enlarge business and make up cargoes. But all these things were supplementary to the Great Five, and an appreciation of this fact at once simplifies and rationalizes the complex story which otherwise is liable to baffle the reader.

Then, again, it may sometimes be worth while to distinguish, where possible, between deliberate, organized long-range trade and what may best be called 'commercial drift'. Trade in the five staple commodities was certainly organized. The *commercia* of the Baltic amber coast, the 'treaty ports' of the Orient, are illustrations, but the matter is not in doubt. How far, on the diplomatic level, the machinery of trade was an affair of the Imperial government, and how far it rested with the individual prestige and experience of the Roman shipping-companies is less certain. In the home waters of the Red Sea, direct government control was exercised; the centurion of Leukē Komē (p. 116) is good proof, and the licensed tax-collector Annius Plocamus exercised rights far round the Arabian coast (p. 128). It may be that the 'Temple of Augustus' at Muziris (p. 121) indicates an official arm long enough to reach the Malabar Coast. But it may also be suspected that much of the more distant negotiation rested with commercial enterprise on a less formal basis, as in the earlier days of the East India Company. The so-called 'embassy' to the Chinese king in A.D. 166 (p. 174) has an unofficial ring about it, in spite of its pretension. And, as we have seen, the presence of sporadic Western goods at Oc-eo in Indo-China suggests mere drift in an intercourse essentially Indian rather than Roman in its structure. To drift likewise may be attributed the pots and coins which straggled on to the high plateau of the central Deccan and were sometimes copied there by local craftsmen. Most of the Roman goods from Free Germany were doubtless the product of drift from market to market or individual to individual, even when all allowance is made for diplomatic gift or military and tribal movement.

Each major discovery during the past 20 years has contributed, not only to the material content of our knowledge, but inferentially to the significant enlargement of our historical perspective in respect of these trans-frontier contacts. In the Fezzan the Germa monument, for all its loneliness or even because of it, has about it the suggestion of something more than casual trading, and has here been recognized tentatively as a relic of a political agency disguised (as so often nowadays) in the shape of a technical mission (p. 106). Arikamedu or Podoukē, on the Bay of Bengal, has shown how, in the time of Augustus and Tiberius, Roman wine and table-wares were already reaching the far-off Coromandel coast in quantity, and the map of early Roman coinage across south India has pointed to the trans-peninsular route whereby they came from the harbours of Muziris or Nelcynda. The Arikamedu excavations have revealed for us how at this time a new commercial and industrial town sprang up here on the site of an insignificant village, and, with the help of the *Periplus* and Ptolemy, have illustrated the astonishing fashion in which under the Principate, the shores of India—eastern no less than western —lit up with the beacons of a new international trade. And the Tamil literature has shown us vividly something of the foreign quarters of these harbour-towns, with their 'abodes of the prosperous Yavanas' and their 'sailors from many lands'. The Yavana sailors must mostly have been Egyptian Greeks and Arabs, but we may suppose that here and there a more or less resident freedman represented the interests of a master sitting afar off in one of the shipping offices of Alexandria or Ostia, Myos Hormos or Berenice. To such accredited freedmen doubtless devolved the patient task of negotiating with local rajas and producers.

Two thousand miles further north, the excavations of Taxila and Begram have produced a different but no less revealing picture: of a rich trade in transit to and from further Asia, shedding samples *en route* in market or douane, but not chaffering to any great extent in these lands of passage. The two famous sites are complementary, and together constitute a formidable addition to the older evidence. Then, finally, the excavations of British, French, Japanese and other archaeologists in Indo-China and central Asia have hinted at possibilities rather than produced finite information. There further evidence must be awaited.

From all this trafficking emerges a question of values which deserves some attention in the long view of history. To what extent were Western *ideas* diffused in the course of this vast diffusion of Western commodities? The importance of trans-frontier trade as a reflection of Roman enterprise and determination is manifest. Had it any more enduring consequence as a social or cultural stimulus in the lands to which it penetrated? More often than not the answer to this question must be 'No'. The Free Germans learned in one way or another to use Roman weapons and equally accustomed the Romans to the use of German or Scythian arms. The glamour of the Roman world, brought to their doors by trade and war, drew the migrating tribes and in some measure directed the refashioning of Europe; but it cannot be said that in its homes Free Germany was greatly influenced by contacts with Roman culture. The restless Garamantes of Africa may have been anchored temporarily in the interests of Rome by an imposed agricultural system and occasional trade, but their romanization, such as it was, had no long-term effect upon the cultures of inner Africa. The far more extensive contacts with South India have been a blessing to the archaeologist in search of fixed points for the dating of associated Indian cultures, but had no appreciable influence upon those cultures themselves. Only in the north, in north-western India (West Pakistan) and Afghanistan, have we found evidences of a fructual contact between West and East. There the combined accidents of the appropriate aesthetic and religious needs of the contemporary Buddhism, of a wealthy and powerful native régime favourable to that Buddhism, and of the diversion of much of the trans-Asian traffic of the West through the region by Parthian intransigence, brought the arts of the Mediterranean and of India together in a rare mutual understanding. ˙Unless it be in the mingling of Muslim and Hindu traits in the medieval architecture of the same sub-continent, it is difficult to find another occasion on which so close an integration of two essentially alien traditions has been achieved. Disputation as to the precise manner of that integration—and disputation will continue until more exact evidence is forthcoming—cannot obscure the magnitude of the fact. And it is tempting to insist rather upon this positive instance of the transmission of ideas than upon the more negative transmission of pots and pence with which the bulk of our study, as of such studies generally, has been concerned.

Outside the immediate range of commercial and cultural values, a brave attempt has been made by an American historian[1] to fasten upon this international trade the responsibility for the major wars and migrations in Europe and Asia during the 1st centuries B.C. and A.D. and, by inference, over an indefinitely larger period. Within a selected time-bracket (58 B.C. to A.D. 107), the writer in question has tabulated, region by region from Britain to Cambodia, the known wars and disturbances, and has observed that every barbarian uprising in Europe followed the outbreak of war either on the eastern frontiers of the Roman Empire or in the 'Western Regions' of the Chinese. What is the significance of this coincidence? It is concluded that the correspondence of wars in the East and the invasions in the West was due to *interruptions of trade*, with Chinese aggression as a primary agency and Roman aggression as a secondary one. 'When war occurred on the routes in the Tarim basin, disturbances broke out in Parthia and either in Armenia or on the border of Syria. Evidently, then, war in the Tarim

[1] F. J. Teggart, *Rome and China* (Univ. of California, 1939).

occasioned an interruption of traffic on the silk route, and this
interruption aroused hostilities at points along the route as
far west as the Euphrates.   It seems highly probable, for
example, that the invasions of Armenia by the Parthians,
while Armenia was controlled by Rome, were inspired by
the suspicion that the Romans had succeeded in diverting
the movement of commodities from Central Asia to some
route which avoided Parthian territory.   But these secondary
or derivative wars . . . brought about new interruptions of
trade, and thus led to new wars in more and more distant
areas.   So interruptions of traffic on the Black Sea stirred up
peoples north of the [lower] Danube, and the long train of
disturbances ended finally in collisions of the barbarians with
the Roman legions on the Rhine.   Consequently, it is to
be seen that people in no way concerned with the Silk
Route might yet be connected with the interruptions of trade
on that route through the hostilities which the interruptions
precipitated between Parthia and Rome. . . .'   In this theory
the Silk Route and its extensions become an instrument of
High Tragedy, of a forthright kind which by its very
simplicity is suspect as an explanation of the complex work-
ings of history.   Other simple solutions of folk-disturbance
have been sought from time to time in factors such as
climatic fluctuation, evolving economy, overcrowding,
personal or national ambition.   These are facets of the
problem, variously emphatic in varying circumstance; they
are not its core, which is likely enough to lie embedded
beyond the superficial view of history.   Amongst them,
trade-routes and commodities may be sufficiently stressed
without the implication that history must be regarded
persistently through a shop window.

N

SELECT BIBLIOGRAPHY

GENERAL

M. P. Charlesworth, *Trade-routes and Commerce of the Roman Empire* (Cambridge, 1926).

EUROPE

O. Brogan, 'Trade between the Roman Empire and the Free Germans', in *the Journal of Roman Studies* XXVI (London, 1936), 195ff.

H. C. Broholm, *Danmark og Romerriget* (Copenhagen, 1952).

H. J. Eggers, *Der römische Import im freien Germanien* (*Atlas der Urgeschichte* I, Hamburg, 1951).

H. Shetelig and H. Falk, *Scandinavian Archaeology* (Oxford, 1937).

AFRICA

G. Caputo and others in *Monumenti Antichi* XLI (Rome, 1951).

M. Reygasse, *Monuments funéraires préislamique de l'Afrique du nord* (Paris, 1950).

ASIA

M. P. Charlesworth, 'Roman Trade with India: a Resurvey', in *Studies in Roman Economic and Social History in Honour of Allan Chester Johnson*, ed. by P. R. Coleman-Norton (Princeton Univ. Press, 1951).

W. W. Tarn, *The Greeks in Bactria and India* (Cambridge, 1951).

E. H. Warmington, *The Commerce between the Roman Empire and India* (Cambridge, 1928).

R. E. M. Wheeler, 'Roman Contact with India, Pakistan and Afghanistan', in *Aspects of Archaeology, Essays presented to O. G. S. Crawford*, ed. by W. F. Grimes (London, 1951).

INDEX

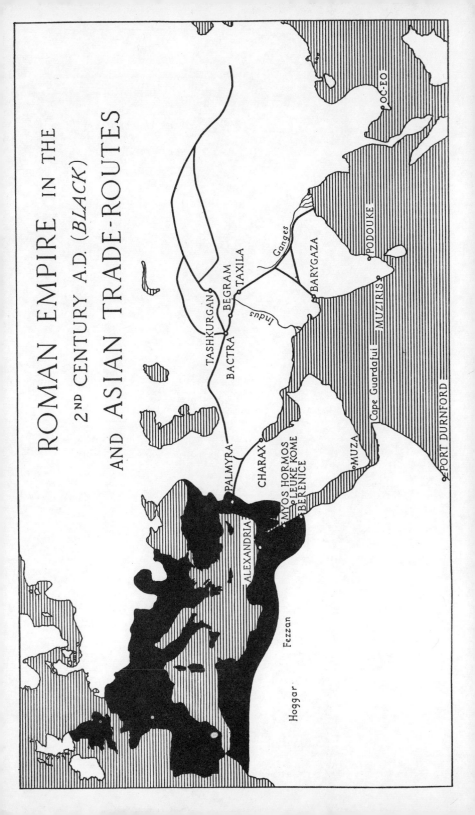

ROMAN EMPIRE IN THE
2ND CENTURY A.D. (*BLACK*)
AND ASIAN TRADE-ROUTES

OC-EO

PODOUKE

TASHKURGAN
BEGRAM
TAXILA
Ganges
BARYGAZA
Indus
BACTRA
MUZIRIS

PALMYRA
Cape Guardafui

CHARAX
MYOS HORMOS
LEUKE KOME
BERENICE
ALEXANDRIA
MUZA
PORT DURNFORD

Fezzan

Hoggar

Do Animals Talk?

by David McCoy

Harcourt

Orlando   Boston   Dallas   Chicago   San Diego

Visit *The Learning Site!*

www.harcourtschool.com

Can you tell when your dog wants something to eat? Have you heard your dog barking at other dogs? Some people think animals communicate through sounds such as barks, meows, chirps, or whistles. Animals may be telling each other that there is trouble ahead. They may be telling each other where to find food. They may simply be letting each other know where they are.

Scientists have tried to find out if animals actually talk to each other. No one knows for sure. As soon as one researcher comes up with proof that animals "talk," another researcher comes along with proof that they don't.

One thing is certain, however. Many animals make unique sounds. A wolf may or may not be "speaking" to another wolf when it howls. A cricket may or may not be chatting with other crickets when it sings. The cricket and the wolf are definitely making sounds, though!

What follows is a look at some of the most interesting noisemakers in the animal kingdom. They include spotted hyenas, vervet monkeys, and humpback whales. You will learn what sounds different animals make and why they make them. You may be surprised at what you find out. You may listen more sympathetically to the sounds around you.

Wolves

If a hungry coyote gets too close to a wolf's food, the wolf snarls and growls. Wolves will not let other animals get close enough to eat any of their food. The coyote may whine wistfully, but it stops scrounging for food near the wolves. It knows that after snarling and growling, wolves attack. However, the sound most often linked with wolves is their howl.

Wolves live in packs of four to twelve or more members. The pack's territory covers about one square mile. Most people who study wolves believe that wolves howl to stake out their territory. The howl tells other animals that this land has been claimed by this pack of wolves.

The pack leader usually starts howling first. Then the other members of the pack join in. Together, the wolves are sending a message to other packs in the area to stay away. If other packs come too close, the wolves might attack. The wolves do not want other wolves to compete with them for food. Some researchers believe that wolves can hear howls from five or more miles away.

Wolves don't usually howl when there are baby wolves in their pack. Some experts believe that the wolves don't want to let their enemies know where their cubs are.

Vervet Monkeys

Researchers believe that vervet monkeys make different calls depending on which type of predator they spot: snakes, mammals, or birds.

These researchers spend months, even years, eavesdropping on groups of monkeys. They keep records of the sounds the vervets make. They also note which call is used to signal each predator. The researchers believe that the monkeys are not just wildly excitable. Their screams mean something.

When a vervet spots a snake, it makes a frantic scream. The other vervets cluster together and stand on their hind legs, looking for the snake. They move slowly away from the snake once they see it.

After seeing a hyena, cheetah, or leopard, a vervet gives a different scream. This scream causes the other monkeys to climb trees. The monkeys move to the ends of thin branches. There they will be safe from a heavy animal. The animal won't be able to climb after them without breaking the branch and falling. The monkeys can also leap from treetop to treetop.

When a vervet monkey sees an eagle, it lets out a third kind of scream. This scream causes the other monkeys to run for cover. The monkeys dive into bushes or huddle near tree trunks, where the eagle won't be able to see them.

Dolphins

Some researchers think that dolphins are very intelligent. They seem to communicate by speaking to one another. Some researchers believe that dolphins can be taught to speak to humans. One researcher taped a dolphin "speaking." Then he played the tape back at a slower speed. He said the dolphin's sounds were like English words!

Studying dolphin sounds is difficult. One problem is that dolphins' sounds are very high pitched. Most of their sounds are not in the hearing range of humans. Humans can hear only a few of the sounds that a dolphin makes.

Most researchers agree that each dolphin in a group has its own special sound. Each dolphin makes a unique whistle. For instance, when a mother dolphin and her baby are separated, the mother calls out with her whistle. The infant responds with its own whistle. Even a baby has its own special signal.

The way dolphins produce sounds is still unknown. Air leaves a dolphin's body through an opening called a blowhole. On its way out, the air passes between two small bumps. Some scientists think the air creates a sound as it passes between these bumps. This is the dolphin's whistle.

Humpback Whales

Perhaps the most complex sound made by any animal in the wild is the song of the male humpback whale. The sounds in this song range from low groans and rumbles to high whistles and rattling shrieks. Many scientists think that each song sends information to other whales. The whales could be identifying their location. They could be challenging other whales. Their songs could be a logical language, for all we know.

At the beginning of the winter mating period, all the male humpbacks in a particular group sing the song from the year before. Then that song begins to change.

After a while the whales are singing a brand new song. Some scientists think whales teach each other their songs.

A whale song lasts ten to fifteen minutes. A researcher once taped a song that was thirty minutes long! To sing, whales have to hold their breath. Some scientists think that whales use songs to see who is strongest. A whale that can sing a longer song might be considered stronger than other whales. It can hold its breath for a longer period of time.

A dolphin may greet an acquaintance with its distinct whistle. It is unclear whether each humpback whale has an identifying song.

Spotted Hyenas

The spotted hyena makes a noise that sounds like a human laugh. This is why they are often called laughing hyenas.

Spotted hyenas hunt in packs of up to thirty animals. The sounds hyenas use include snorts, grunts, and giggles. These sounds communicate different kinds of information. They allow the hyenas to work together efficiently. As a result, hyenas are skillful hunters.

Once a hyena catches its prey—such as a vervet monkey—it tells the rest of its pack about it. The hyena uses various sounds, including its famous laugh.

Mockingbirds

There are thousands of different species of birds. Each type of bird has its own song. One of the most interesting singers is the mockingbird. A mockingbird sings only the songs of other birds. It will often sing the same short song two or three times in a row. Then it will copy the song of another bird. Unless you listen for a while, it may be hard to tell you are listening to a mockingbird.

Some researchers believe that the mockingbird can copy the songs of twenty or more species within ten minutes. Most mockingbirds know the songs of twenty-five to thirty other birds.

Crickets

Most of the animals mentioned so far will not keep you up at night—unless you happen to live in the woods or in the middle of the ocean.

However, you might have fallen asleep to the sounds of one common insect, the cricket. It sometimes sounds as if every cricket in your neighborhood is chirping away at the same time. This is not the case.

First, only male crickets chirp. A cricket chirps by rubbing two of its smaller wings together. A series of chirps is called a trill. The male cricket chirps and trills to attract females. It also chirps to tell other males to go away.

Second, male crickets take turns making noise. If two males start calling at the same time, one stops chirping and moves farther away. The male cricket can choose when, where, and how loud to chirp.

Researchers have determined that humans can hear only part of a cricket's trill. Crickets make some sounds that are higher pitched than our ears can hear. The sounds we cannot hear are actually the most important part of the cricket's song. However, scientists have been able to tell crickets apart just by studying the sounds humans can hear.

Animal	Sound
Wolf 	Howl
Vervet monkey	Scream
Dolphin	Whistle
Humpback whale	Groan, whistle, shriek

Animal	Sound
Spotted hyena	Laugh
Mockingbird	Other birds' songs
Cricket	Chirp